The Turning Point

The Turning Point

to Being, Awareness, Joy

Douglas Harding

The Shollond Trust

Published by The Shollond Trust

87B Cazenove Road

London N16 6BB England

headexchange@gn.apc.org

www.headless.org

The Shollond Trust is a UK charity, reg. no 1059551

This book was typed up by the following volunteers. The Shollond Trust is extremely grateful to them for their help:

Al Matanovic, Axel Tanner, Barbara Becker, Bill Gillies , Bruce Wilding, Carolann Sharp, Cathy Christian, Chris Owen, Damien Thomas, Danielle Bol-De-Greve, Dave Croce, David A. Burnet, Helen Connor, Howard Davies, Jane Jannotta, Janet Cook, Jenny Legge, Jim Van Meggelen, John Boynton, Julie Hawkins, Julie Pogachefsky, Kevin Michael, Kevin Young, Laudis Rodriguez, Mary M. Walsh, Melanie Gamble, Michael Haederle, Miguel Angel Sosa Cravioto, Nelly Beraud Edmeads, Nick Cramp, Nina Finnigan, Rakshita-Athalia, Richard Lang, Rob Vlaar, Roy Potter, Shane Keher, Stephanie Klauser, Toby Philpott, Wilf Gotham.

This book is the third collection of essays by Douglas Harding, coming after Look For Yourself and To Be And Not To Be. (The fourth collection, As I See It, gathers up all the remaining essays by Harding that are not otherwise in print so that, as of 2018, all Harding's essays are now available.)

Contents

FOREWORD

This book has three essential components. (1) A lot of words, plus the points they make. (2) Pictures and diagrams of mine to help make sense of those points. (3) Half a dozen experiments or tests or exercises designed to reveal what you can *see* you are, in sharp distinction from what you think you are and are told you are. These experiments are the backbone of the whole. I can't stress too strongly that they are for *doing,* and just reading about them is worse than useless. Yes, much worse!

Because each chapter is self-contained and complete in itself you can read them in any order you like. But this does mean that you will find a good deal of verbal repetition, and instructions to repeat experiments that you have already done. For this I make no apology. They *are* for repetition, and can't be done too often. In fact, they are for doing till they come so naturally that it's as if they do themselves.

Two more pieces of advice about how to read this book. (1) If you are new to the "headless way" I urge you to read the chapters in the order printed. They do build up to a climax. (2) Since at Root every chapter is about the same Thing—or, rather No-thing—it matters little if you find some chapters obscure or incomprehensible. Just read on, and you will come to other parts of the book that are quite clear and easy going. Take for instance the last chapter entitled I AM: some friends find it far too complex, while others don't. But I'm sure that all my "headless" friends will come across frequently in this book the Great Simplification that works wonders.

I conclude on a warning note—to believe anything you read in this book without testing it to the limit *is to condemn yourself to bondage and slavery.* As Nicolai Berdyaev tells us: "God has laid on mankind the duty of being free, no matter how difficult that may be, or how much suffering that may involve." This sounds much more miserable than it is, seeing that in fact this is the only real freedom, as well as the unfailing cure for suffering and the sure recipe for divine and lasting joy.

D. E. Harding

I dedicate this book to my wife Catherine, who so helpfully examined and passed every chapter, without necessarily agreeing with all of it. She's French, and for the French, of course, liberty comes first, before equality and fraternity.

1. LET'S GROW UP

Man is a shocking case of arrested development.

When not cut short, our life is a four-stage affair.

First, the new-born baby who has no boundaries.

Second, the child who some of the time agrees with grown-ups that the object in the mirror is himself, while the rest of the time he's still boundless.

Third, the adult who has lost his space and become his face. Almost all of us are stuck at this stage. We substitute the dying thing we look like over there for the deathless no-thing we are here, thereby condemning ourselves to death and fear, hate, greed, and delusion.

Fourth, to grow up we must turn our attention round 180° and *look at* What we're *looking out of.* Then we rediscover the clarity and immensity we enjoyed as infants, and find that we are, in all vital respects, the *opposite* of what we look like. In particular, we find that the face-to-face confrontation of Stage Three is a lie and that we all are disappearing in one-another's favour.

Our job is to live this way, and so help Man grow up.

I'm not suggesting that the third and desperately difficult stage of our life can be dispensed with, but it needs cutting down. The longer it drags on the harder it gets to stop. Seventeen is a good age for discovering you are still space for the world to happen in.

Few reach this Fourth Stage, and the ability of those who do so to change the world seems negligible. The individual seems powerless, but before giving up hope, let's face what our Fourth Stage amounts to. It's the realization that by grace you and I are One with our Source, identical at Centre with the Power that's giving rise to Itself, plus all things from quarks to galaxies, and that we aren't through to the One as human beings, but as the One, as the only Real Power.

There's an early Buddhist story that the Buddha's enlightenment ensured the enlightenment of all sentient beings. I'm saying that when you see into your boundless, immaculate, imperishable, all-inclusive, wide-awake Nature and Source and Centre, you do so as One with and empowered by the only Real and Ultimate Power that, having already achieved the "impossible" miracle of Self-origination, isn't easily baffled. Tell me, what's impossible for the One that creates Itself? And what's impossible for those who enjoy union with that One?

Man has survived ice-ages, ages of stagnation, every sort of nastiness and nonsense. It's up to us, who see that we are by grace One with the One, to see our brothers and sisters through to the love and the glory that shines here at the heart of All.

You can't grow up apart from them, for the simple reason that to get Home to the One as the One you must take with you, piggyback, all that comprise the One.

2. WHAT'S GONE WRONG?

Few people would agree with Robert Browning's rapturous cry that all's right with the world. Most of us, most of the time, feel that something's terribly amiss. The aim of this chapter is to find out what it is that has gone wrong, and what—if anything—you and I can do about it. An ambitious project! Yes indeed! But let's see how far we can get.

We need hardly bother to list the things about ourselves and the world that we don't like, that aren't as they should be. They are too many and too obvious. So let's move straight on to consider the various ways we can and do respond to the troubles that threaten to engulf us.

As I see it, we have four alternatives, the first of which is—

Resentment

And a very natural reaction it is! We had no choice, no say at all, in the sex and temperament and appearance and social status and circumstances imposed upon us. We weren't consulted about when and where we were flung into the world and what kind of world it was and is. Our preferences and needs were—it seems—unfeelingly ignored. We were pitchforked into this blood-soaked arena which, apparently, is all set up to hurt and mangle and soon destroy us. What sort of Creator or Demiurge is it (we want to know) who gives us one nature, and along with it all sorts of frustrations and contradictions of that nature? Who gives us, so to speak, a nature and an anti-nature, who actually fixes it up that whereas we need

3

love and security and success and joy and peace, most of the time we get their opposites? What have innocent babies done to deserve all the pain and disillusion, ending in sickness and senility and death itself, that is steadily coming to them? Surely the only appropriate reaction is anger.

But the trouble with anger is that it's unproductive. It's a dead end, and gets us nowhere at all. It only piles on the agony.

Resignation

Is the second alternative and it is rather less negative. Thus we say to ourselves, wryly but sensibly, "Life is difficult." Or, with the Buddha, "Life is painful, life is suffering." So, let's stop pretending that it could be otherwise than tragic, terribly unfair, made up of anxiety upon anxiety, agony piled on agony. Let's nobly face the noble but dreadful truth that our world (including ourselves, of course) is a Divine Tragedy and by no means a Divine Comedy, even for the lucky ones. Lucky for how long? Or a very Black Comedy, if you prefer to put it like that.

There is a positive side to this hard-boiled realism. It makes a difference when at last we give up all our false optimism and wishful thinking, our pathetic pretence that tomorrow or next week or next year things will be back to normal, and happy days (well, happier days) will be here again. Suffering is the rule, relief from suffering the exception. Grant that tomorrow's trials may well be at least as severe as today's, and a certain peace does descend upon us now we are honest enough to acknowledge the grim facts, steadily and

4

without bitterness. Life can become somewhat more bearable, less of a let-down—provided we are sufficiently stoical.

Submission

Is our third alternative. Saying to God, and meaning what we say: "Not my will but thine be done."

Of course this alignment of our will with His will is pleasant and easy when all goes fairly well with us, very hard when things go badly, next to impossible (unless we are already saints) when disaster threatens and our very lives are at stake. Even Jesus was agonisingly torn between his own will and his Father's in the end. And if even he found this ultimate surrender immensely difficult when it came to the crunch, what hope for us ordinary mortals? What hope for me, I should say. You may be a great saint, for all I know.

Yet most if not all of the world's great spiritual leaders tell us that here lies the answer to our troubles. If only we could be selfless, totally surrendered! There's the rub. Real saints are extremely rare. How many of us are able and willing to transcend and do violence to our deep-seated instinct for survival? To immolate ourselves, to play the part of the priest that sacrifices and of the sacrifice itself. And to do so not merely because in the end it's the best policy, but because it's the only right thing to do?

The answer, of course, is very, very few of us. And even that heroic few, who by virtue of Grace or extraordinary feats of discipline and self-abnegation, manage genuinely to will God's will as it impinges on their own lives—even they do not necessarily find that the Universe is, after all, a consistently happy and beautiful place. With some exceptions, they don't see it that way at all. No. The saints are apt to embrace the world in spite of what it is rather than because of what it is. Some of them haven't a good word to say for it.

And so, on the face of it, there's no feasible solution, for us unsaintly ones, to the problem of what's gone wrong with the world we are part of. We have seen that *raging* against things only makes matters worse, that *resignation,* though extremely difficult, may help us somewhat but does little to improve the situation, and that full *acceptance* or *surrender* is virtually impossible for us as we are now.

However, there is a fourth alternative, so let's take heart and go into it carefully and critically and with open minds. After all what have we—desperate characters that we are, in a desperate situation—to lose?

Here is a very different approach from the three we have outlined. I trust you will find that it does hold out hope—even certainty—for us rather ordinary people, provided we are willing to drop some of our precious opinions and dare to take a fresh look at ourselves and the world we find ourselves in.

The proposition we are going to examine is this: *In itself, the world is alright. It isn't the world that has gone wrong, or is unsatisfactory, but what you and I are all the time doing to it.*

Or let me put it like this. Apart from us the Universe would be alive and in great shape; it is we who are the trouble. We are inflicting a grievous wound upon it.

We have split it into two unequal fragments called ME and NOT-ME, or OURSELF and THE REST. The result is that we don't live in a Universe, but a Duoverse, which is a very uncomfortable place to find oneself stuck in. And it's hardly surprising that each of the two severed parts of the Whole should be sick for the lack of the other. Tragically and incurably sick, so long as that gaping wound isn't closed and healed.

Now look at the *shape* of the wound. It penetrates to the very Heart of the One. Why am I sure of this? Because at Root all of us who say "I AM this or that or the other" do so by virtue of our basic identity with the One. Yes, strictly speaking, we are a gang of suicidal deicides!

The *Katha Upanishad* diagnoses the disease: "He who divides the One wanders from death to death." And prescribes the remedy: "Tell the mind there is but One." And the Third Patriarch of Zen speaks of the health which that remedy brings: "When the Ten Thousand things are viewed in their Oneness, we are returned to the Origin and remain where we have always been... One in All, All in One—if only this is realised, no more worry about not being perfect."

But again, merely understanding and concurring with the Oneness doesn't get us far along the difficult road to perfection. Sure enough, when times are fairly good and the sun's shining and the birds are singing, it's not too difficult to feel the Oneness of all things, with ourselves caught up in the Grand Design. Or maybe when meditating in the tranquillity of a holy place.

Thus we may occasionally sense that, however miserable the parts of the world may be as parts, the Whole is at this very moment all that our hearts could possibly wish for. Just as the most horrible slum, viewed from a weather satellite, becomes a thing of beauty, and our sad, war-torn planet, viewed from the Moon, becomes a shining monument to peace—so when we are in exalted mood, our ambiguous Universe may briefly be viewed in its wholeness as wholly good. When we are in the mood! How are we to live in that exalted and rarefied atmosphere for more than a few moments at a time? Someone has described life here on Earth as one of quiet desperation. I guess he was right except that I would call it noisy desperation. "Some day," says Master K'ung Ku Chin-lung, "you will recognise that the Serene Land of Pure Light is none other than the Earth itself." Meanwhile you may—if you are fortunate—enjoy that realisation in flashes. The rest of the time this Earth is with reason described by Mrs Gamp as "a wale of tears."

So what is our practical answer? I have already suggested that it is a very simple one—simple, if not exactly easy. *So long as I am anything whatever I have divided and so spoiled the One.*

The only remedy is to restore the property I stole, to re-graft the organ I had amputated, to claim Nothing—and so bring Everything to life, health, and wholeness. "Claim Nothing, enjoy. Do not covet His property," says the *Isa Upanishad*. In ancient China, around the same time, the Taoist sage Chuang-tzu had this to say: "Your body is not your own. It is the delegated image of God. Your life is not your own. It is the delegated harmony of God. Your individuality is not your own. It is the delegated adaptability of God." And, two millennia later, the French Jesuit Jean Pierre de Caussade (1675–1751) wrote: "The body and its senses, the soul and its energies, the modicum of good you have performed, are God's portion. It so manifestly belongs to Him that you realize that you cannot claim one whit of it as yours, nor feel one grain of complacency, *without being guilty of theft and larceny from God*." Another Jesuit, John Nicholas Grou, (1731–1803), having pointed out how God is All and the creature is Nothing, goes on to say, "I am nothing of myself and owe to God all that I am... If I appropriate these gifts to myself I steal from Him what is His own, I commit an injustice." Karl Marx, too, attacking injustice, decided that all property is theft, but didn't go far enough. He excluded such personal property as clothes and cooking utensils, and of course one's body and mind. He had the right idea, but stopped short of the heart of the matter. No wonder Marxism doesn't set our world to rights. It's far from radical enough.

So I admit I'm a thief, a despoiler of the world. Thieves, however, are loath to part with their loot, specially when they have held onto it for so long that they have come to regard it as their very own, and a lot of people have agreed with them. Who of us is prepared to return his body-mind to the Universe, and be reduced to *absolute poverty?*

The only convincing reason that I can find for this restoration of stolen goods to their rightful Owner—the only consideration that would induce me to hand them over willingly and without delay—would be the clear perception that I have no choice, seeing that they were never mine anyway, and my thieving was quite imaginary. In other words, if I were actually to see, and not just believe that right here there is No-thing whatever, and that where there is No-thing there is No-problem. Then this clear seeing into my non-existent self would certainly loosen my grip on that pseudo-self.

Well, in sharpest contrast to the achievement of sainthood, this clear seeing is available on demand, as easy as winking, a piece of cake, the gracious and wholly undeserved and indestructible gift of a merciful God and loving Saviour. In fact, the awesome truth is that this Central No-thing is not only the ineffable Source of all those peripheral things but far more brilliantly on display than any of them. Only This can be perfectly seen because only This is perfectly simple!

Still I ask myself: Is it *true* that I'm not the body and mind I thought I was? And everyone told me I was. Is it a hard fact that I am in reality No-thing whatever, and that I neither have nor am so much as a dust-grain? Or is this just holy talk, pious uplift, a good thing to believe because it makes me more comfortable? I must find out because only complete honesty with myself will work here. A trace of wishful thinking, and this promising recipe for trouble does me and my world no good at all.

Well, I can't speak for you of course, but I do indeed find that this Nothingness—this absence of body-mind right here—is the most obvious of all obvious truths. Whether I like it or not, I see, far more clearly than I see anything out there in the world, that right here is Emptiness, Space, Openness, Vacant Accommodation for the whole astonishing Set-up. Whenever I look back here at what's looking, look once more at this mysterious Spot I'm said to occupy, I find it unoccupied by me—I see that I am No-thing, and occupied instead by all sorts of things. Right here I'm just Capacity, Room at this moment for these two arms and hands, this busy pen, this half-filled sheet of paper, this littered desk-top, and beyond them the window and the view, grass and bare trees and racing clouds and cold sky. Plus all sorts of thoughts and feelings about these and other things. I am nowhere to be found, and everywhere. I have no body and the whole world is my Body, I'm at once Nothing and All things, and never, never am something. There's no compromise, no half-way house between these extremes. That great poet and saint St. John of the Cross tells me that to be all things I must be nothing, but I don't have to take his word for it. I can always check this astounding fact, whatever my mood or activity of the moment, just by taking a look at what I'm looking out of right here.

Don't tell me you can't see at your own very Centre exactly What I'm telling you about. You are now looking at these lines of black printing on white paper. What, at this moment and on present evidence, is taking them in right where you are? No-one is in a position to say but you. You are the sole and final authority on what you are now looking out of, on what's going on at the very Centre of your world. Has it any colour? Has it any size or shape or texture? If so, what? Is it one of those things? If so, it must be getting in the way of this printing.

I ask you: isn't it precisely the *ABSENCE* of all things, a boundless and perfectly blank screen, so to say, which is in receipt of these printed words, and of whatever else happens to be on offer? A No-thing that's *awake* to its no-thingness? Now that, you may be tempted to say, is Quite Something!

Nevertheless you ask me: "How on Earth can I see an absence, something that isn't there to see?"

I reply: you can and you do so, with the greatest of ease, all the time. As I have already pointed out, whereas *things* are more or less inscrutable because they are so complicated, their *absence* is vividly on show because it's so simple. For example, my absence from the room you are now sitting in is at once crystal-clear to you, but if I were present you would only be able to *glimpse* me. Why? Why because to take all of me in—every tint and line and hair and blemish and so forth, from hair-do to chin, and from chin to shoe-soles, would be impossible. What you actually *see* of me is a tiny fraction of what's there for the seeing—not to mention the view from above and the sides and the back and the innumerable details of my interior anatomy. Truly I'm the Invisible Man! You don't *smell* my absence (I hope). You see it, just as you see the absence of a misprint (I hope) from this page.

"All the same," I hear you saying, "I *feel* I am this body that sits in this chair and talks to people and walks around the room."

Then your feelings (I reply) are playing you up. What is this little body of yours without all its ingredients of every grade down to and beyond quark? You aren't human without the other humans, or alive without the other species, or existent without your planet and star. Indeed the whole strictly indivisible Cosmos is your true Body, and nothing less will do. In other words, you are the Nothing that's all the while exploding into the All, the One. And in yet other words you are, by the free Grace of that One, indissolubly united to that One. You appear to be human but are really No-thing and Every-thing. And your trouble is that you don't see that when you say, "After all, I'm only human," you are talking the most arrant and damaging nonsense.

Speaking for myself again, this clear perception of my Nothingness, carrying with it utter conviction, is my best hope and indeed only hope of setting things to rights. Let me go on seeing what I am at Centre, how everything I had supposed I was, everything I had stolen, is already restored to its Owner, and see what happens as a result. Insofar as I do just this I do indeed find that all's healed and made whole.

And I see that, while I'm wholly unable to make myself into any kind of *saint* (and try to settle the world's problems that immensely difficult way), I'm also wholly unable to make myself into any sort of *person,* let alone a good one. And that will have to do. This in-seeing is easy, natural, refreshing, secular, not special at all. Not so easy to keep up all the while without a good deal of practice, no doubt, but renewable always and at will, whenever I choose to turn my attention round to the Absence of any attender right here.

So this, our fourth alternative, is certainly the one for me. What about you? If you tell me this No-thingness looks so boring, so dull and seemingly quite useless, I'll agree. But you and I have a precious secret reason for refusing to rubbish it like this. Let me explain. You are made of cells, which are creatures capable of exerting a lot of force, such as splitting rocks and lifting paving stones. And the cells are made of molecules which (as gun-powder, for instance) can exert much greater force. And the molecules in turn are made of atoms which (as in the atom bomb) are very much more powerful and of course much dirtier. And the atoms are made of particles which (as in the nuclear bomb) are still more powerful and dirty. And the particles are made of the No-thing that you and I find at our very Centre—the No-thing that gives rise to All things. And is hiddenly all-powerful and absolutely clean. In the last resort, nothing but This is trustworthy. It's also perfectly verifiable, actual-factual, not for taking on trust just because you read about It somewhere, or because somebody calling himself *reverend* told you so. You certainly shouldn't believe me when I say that you, too, are likely to find the world radically transformed once you clearly see for yourself that you can never steal so much as a needle from it. Just give your boundless Central Clarity a fighting chance to reveal itself and see what happens.

I say a needle because it brings me to this chapter's conclusion, which is a Muslim tradition about Jesus. The Sufi poet Attar tells the story. "When you are reduced to ashes, including your baggage, you will have not the least feeling of existence. But if there remains to you, as to Jesus, only a simple needle, a hundred thieves will lie in wait for you along the road. Although Jesus had thrown down his baggage, the needle was still able to scratch his face."

Let go! You have nothing to lose, everything to gain!

And, in case it will help to distil this complicated and wordy chapter down to its 100%-proof quintessence, it is this—*Where there's no thing there's no problem.*

3. HOME BY PIGGYBACK

The meaning and purpose of my life is conscious union with its Divine Source. Of course I'm a human being still, but it's way off-Centre and peripheral to the true me by a metre, more or less. Here at my Centre is the Home of the One I really am, of the One who is All.

In order for the One who is All to take up residence here at my Centre that Centre must be quite empty of all things. The slightest thing remaining here in His way would be enough to crowd Him out, and also be enough to reduce Him to less than the All. The blessed fact that He is in me as the Whole of His indivisible Self means that I am Home with Him and as Him, and absolutely free here of the countless imperfections of that peripheral human. Right here and right now I am absolutely cleansed of all my human guilt and weaknesses. What a mercy!

It also means that I can't come Home without you!

Why?

For the simple reason that the All which I am here includes you, along with all the others. Regardless of whether you are aware of the fact or consent to it, every time I come Home it is with you as my piggyback. There's no other way. What's more, no-one can come Home without giving me a piggyback. No credit to you or me or anybody else. By divine grace we are built like that because, as partakers in the Divine Nature, we are One with God *The* Piggybacker.

In their very different ways the great spiritual traditions have announced this marvellously heart-warming and encouraging truth.

Here are two of them.

There is an early Buddhist teaching that, when Gautama saw into his True Nature and became the Buddha, his enlightenment necessarily involved the enlightenment of all sentient beings, past, present and future. Which includes, of course, you and me. Now there's piggybacking on the grandest scale, all right!

At the very heart of Christian faith is the belief that God, in the Person of His Son, has at great cost already saved us all from ourselves and granted us the sure and glorious prospect of total union with Him. All we have to do is say Yes! In other words, to accept His offer of a piggyback Home. So with Paul I say: "I live, yet not I, but Christ lives in me." Christ the Good Shepherd, who seeks and finds the lost sheep and carries it into the sheepfold. And who of us isn't a lost sheep?

I happen to be writing this on the bank of the River Orwell in Suffolk, which George Orwell named himself after. You will remember how grimly his novel *Nineteen Eighty-Four* ends—

Under the spreading chestnut tree
I sold you and you sold me.

I say: in this Third Millenium we have a choice—Shall we carry on like that, or live like this:

Under the spreading Bodhi tree
I bear you and you bear me
Home by piggyback?

4. THE EXPERIENCE AND THE MEANING

"We had the experience but missed the meaning." T. S. Elliot

Introduction

I can't read this well-known line from T. S. Elliot's *The Four Quartets* without adding, mentally, "Or perhaps we had the meaning but missed the experience." We may be suffering from the first deficiency disease or the second—or possibly from both. And most likely with no clear idea of what's the matter.

Hence this chapter. I propose, having sharply distinguished what I take to be the essential Experience from what I take to be its Meaning, to enquire what it is to have either one of them without the other, and what can be done to correct this condition. How (I shall be asking) can we recognise and overcome this imbalance? For who wants to live this way—to live (you might say) a half-life? I have the feeling that a man hopping on one leg or a bird with a broken wing is less crippled, less stuck. But let's see.

The Experience

First, then, let's be clear about what the Experience really, really is.

Three words cover it—*seeing our Nothingness*. It's that simple. Or, to drive the point home, *turning our attention round 180° and looking into What we are looking out of, into our Absence, our Void Nature or Emptiness or Speckless Clarity, into our lack of characteristics, distinguishing marks, attainments, you-name-it.* It is not—emphatically not—knowing all about our Natureless Nature, or understanding it profoundly, or believing in it sincerely, or even feeling it acutely, but seeing it with such finality and such intimacy that we not only *see* this Absence which we are, but *are* this Absence which we see. But alas, how liable even the most apt words are to complicate what is, after all, Simplicity itself?

Strictly speaking, this Experience, which is none other than the substratum of all experience, is impossible to describe. It's as ineffable and incommunicable as the redness of red or the sweetness of honey or the smell of wild violets. Try telling a man colour-blind from birth what purple is. Well, telling him about his Empty Core is even more futile. Somehow you must get him to look in for himself at himself by himself instead of just out at you. Then and only then nothing could be easier or plainer, more blazingly self-evident to him, than his Nothingness, his disappearance in your favour. "Indeed" as the *Sutralamkara* says, "the saving truth has never been preached by the Buddha, seeing that one has to realise it within oneself."

However, four things can be said, and need to be said here, about this essential In-seeing.

First, precisely because it's void of all qualities of its own, because there's Nothing to it, it is for all beings of all grades One and the Same. There are no special angles or perspectives on This, no variations. There are no preliminary or private views or privileged showings, no more enlightened or less enlightened versions of This, no heights to mount to or fall away from, and certainly no religious or spiritual or aesthetic qualities to cultivate.

Second, (and for the same reason) one's "first fleeting glimpse" of one's Nature doesn't differ at all from one's latest and clearest and most sustained seeing" of that Nature. No matter how brief or how sustained it may be, this Experience is unique among all experiences in that it has no degrees of clarity or intensity or familiarity. It's as if every time it happens were the first time. Like it or lump it, there's no encouraging upturn, never any progress to plot on one's spiritual progress chart. Either you see This or you don't. Here's the one skill you can't get better at, but only exercise more frequently and for longer periods.

Third, it follows that, whoever and wherever and whenever you may be, your Inside Story is the plainest of all plain tales, and identical with the Inside Story of all creatures. So that to see What you really are is not only to see What they really are but to be What they really are. Beyond all doubt you are me and him and her and it, and all the rest. And at once you have hit on the answer to all the loneliness and alienation in the world. You rest on the Ground of Being and of all loving and caring. Secretly you are healing, along with your own wounds, the wounds of this wounded world.

Fourth, while no doubt there are, inhabiting countless solar systems in this vast Cosmos, all manner of sentient beings whose bodies differ fantastically from ours, we here who see into our True Nature see equally into their's, and are One with the One in them all.

The Meaning

Notice how the foregoing observations, along with all observations whatever about the Experience, belong to its Meaning, and none of them to the Experience itself. And how there's no way through from the one to the other. Not even the most accurate and profound description of What you really are can give a clue to What you really are, any more than the letters R E D can give a clue to what redness is. Anything that can be said about the Experience—anything having any content or conveying any information—is light-years adrift from the thing itself, and quite incapable of hinting at what it's like. In fact it's like nothing whatever because it is Nothing whatever. Or let's say No-thing whatever, inasmuch as a Nothing *keenly aware of itself as No-thing* is surely more wonderful than the most wonderful Some-thing. And there's no creeping or edging up to this wonderful No-thing. Only a sudden, unpremeditated quantum leap will see you over from what's about you to what is you, to your Void Nature.

Of course the four items of meaning which we have looked at so far are only a tiny sample of its inexhaustible significance and consequences, of its practical applications to all the changing circumstances of our life. Here are a few more—

Whereas the Experience of our nature is served up (if at all) complete in one infinitely generous helping, its Meaning is for the most part withheld. Normally it's doled out in driblets, at other times poured out more generously, but never given in its entirety. The last word about This is never said, the ultimate and all-embracing idea of It is never conceived, the deepest feeling never plumbed. Not that one is complaining. On the contrary, it's a matter of continual admiration and thankfulness that such Poverty should produce such ever-appreciating wealth, that this most negligible and neglected of Seeds should burgeon into this most lasting and prolific of hardy perennials. Thus to have both the Experience and the Meaning is to make the best of both worlds. Improbably, you have it both ways: the ever-present and uneventful safety of Home *and* endless adventure abroad, the Anchor holding you fast to the rock-bottom security of your Ground *and* high winds and taut sails carrying you forever to new adventures.

One of the most notable aspects of this dichotomy—of the total contrast between the Experience and its Meaning—is that whereas the latter is by no means available on demand the former is always available. Once you have hit on the way Home you can take it instantly and at will. No matter how dubious your past or difficult your present or daunting your future, no matter how black your mood or worrying your problems, your right of entry and ease of entry are assured unconditionally. When you most need to go in you can go in—in to the Place you never left. The *Meaning* of what you are doing may or may not occur to you. If it does, be sure that it's provisional and partial and far from all there. But also be sure that the doing itself is perfect, forever unobstructed, opportune, natural, and scot-free. How immensely more triumphant this Homecoming is than all the other things you and I get up to!

On the one hand, the Meaning of your Void Nature—its implications and applications, its endless complications and connections—have to be worked at assiduously. The Meaning takes all the intelligence and energy you can give it, and even so is shy and fugitive, never crystal clear, never quite obvious, never free of contradictions. On the other hand, the Experience of your Nature is always transparent and complete. In fact, till you see What you are you don't know what obviousness is! Only you—the real You, you as you are for you, intrinsically—are absolutely visible. All else is more or less veiled. Compared with this Sight all other sights are obscure, fuzzy, groping, dim. There's something unique about its obviousness, a sharpness, a surprise, a quiet thrill or *frisson* that there's no proper word for.

And all this in spite of its unspeakable ordinariness!

The Experience Without The Meaning

So much, then, for our small sample of the endless distinctions between the Experience and its Meaning. Let's go on now to discover what it is to have the former without the latter.

"That won't be easy," I hear you saying.

To which I reply: it may prove all-too-easy. But let's see.

Look at anyone in the room or at your face in the mirror, and check that you are empty for it, that at this moment you experience yourself as the Space that's taking it in.

Now look at this face that I've drawn.

And check that, *on present evidence,* the set-up is altogether asymmetrical. Notice how his or her face over there is presented to your No-face here, those two little eyes to your single and immense "Eye" here, that patterned opacity to this patternless Transparency, that smallness to this Immensity.

Notice how you can never for a moment confront anyone, never get face-to-face with anyone. Notice how you aren't a bit what you look like to them—people over there being too far off and in no position to see What you really are where you really are. Notice how you can not only see what you are looking at but also (and much more clearly) What you are looking out of.

Some call It your Original Face, others your Buddha Eye, others the Light that lights all who come into the world, yet others your

No-head. But whatever you happen to call It, This is no passing impression or replica of It but the real article, exactly as the Buddha and Jesus and all the other Seers experienced It.

Go on looking in, as well as out, a few more moments, please.

"Why should I bother?" you ask me.

I'll tell you. Because this is the most momentous Experience you or anyone ever had. Because—in spite of its dreadfully boring plainness (you can see It has Nothing whatever to recommend it)—this is the sight of a lifetime, of all lifetimes.

"It's a sight that leaves me cold," I hear you replying. "All it means to me is that of course I can't see my own eyes and face and head. So what? What has it to do with the Buddha's full and perfect enlightenment? Or with the enlightenment I'm working towards and hope to arrive at one day—perhaps many years from now, but more likely many lifetimes from now? Yes of course I see exactly what you mean. But again, *SO WHAT?*"

So there you are! That's it! *There's your Meaningless Experience for you!*

We live in a democracy. Put to the vote, your reaction is the right one. Subject to minor variations, it's what the majority of the population as well as the majority of serious seekers—disciples of the Masters, followers of the great spiritual disciplines—have been telling me over the past few decades. Whenever I got them to reverse their attention and examine the Spot they occupy (only to discover it's not they who occupy it but the others), their comment has been the equivalent of *SO WHAT?* I should say that, at a guess, of a hundred who are persuaded to look in and briefly lose track of themselves, not more than three or four find that their discovery is so surprising and meaningful that it merits cultivation. Even fewer go on valuing and renewing this Insight till it occurs naturally and without prompting, and its life-changing power—its incredible know-how—is revealed.

But no wonder the essential Experience is dismissed so cavalierly, is so unwelcome and so distrusted. The famous *Diamond Sutra* has good reason to warn us that, below the surface, we are all terrified of our Emptiness. Till its inexhaustible and breathtaking beneficence and fertility begin to take shape it must seem to very many of us not just meaningless but suicidal, mere annihilation.

The Meaning Without The Experience

We come now to the other sort of one-sidedness, which would seem to be even more crippling. A heart without a body can be induced to go on working, but a body without a heart??? Well, once more, let's see.

But first let's be clear about one thing. We are not going to take samples of *people* who alas have the Meaning without the Experience, or the body (so to say) without the heart. We shall be looking at occasions or contexts, moods, conversations, lectures, books, in which those people have every appearance of being like that. For it's never perfectly safe to argue from what someone says to what he really means by it, from what he's coming out with to what he's coming from, from one occasion or period of his life to the rest of it. People aren't that consistent or simple. Of no-one would I say that he always lacks access to his Void Nature, or to its significance and power, any more than I would say that he never does so, and has access to both all the time.

For many years, I've admired the writings of a number of contemporary and recent pundits, spiritual experts whose grasp of the Meaning of our True Nature is quite wonderful. The scope and thoroughness of their work is such that it reads as complete. In fact I have found little or nothing in it to fault, and much instruction. The only thing I miss is the Experience. Here's a fine *yana* or vehicle, a splendid chariot and charioteer all right; but in the unforgettable words of the poet Roy Campbell, *where's the bloody horse?*

Mind you, I'm not accusing these experts of setting out to put the cart before the horse, still less of trying to do without the animal altogether. I'm not saying that they have no Experience whatever of their Void Nature, but that they fail to lead me to it and rub my nose (what nose?) in it. Worse, they are apt (no doubt unintentionally) to drag me away from it, as from some perilous cliff-edge or poisoned well. More and more thirsty, I find myself invited to a nine-course banquet of Meaning without a drop of the wine of Experience to wash it down. Naturally I get indigestion, or worse.

To illustrate these remarks the three well-known teachers I'm about to quote will do admirably. You can probably fill in with others from your own shelves.

My first illustrates how ingenious are the dodges by which, given half a chance, we manage to overlook our Original Face; the subterfuges by which we contrive *almost* to see into our Void Nature (and even to extract some minor psychological advantages from the ploy) while remaining safely blind to its blazing obviousness. How cleverly—and stupidly—we set up the idea of it to mask the reality, its usefulness to degrade it into a convenient fiction. You could call this the As-if method of evading What's-so. I quote from a chapter ominously entitled "The Guillotine Meditation".

"One of the most beautiful tantra meditations: walk and think that the head is no more there, just the body. Sit and think that the head is no more there, just the body. Continually remember that the head is not there. Visualise yourself without the head. Have a picture of yourself enlarged without the head; look at it. Let your mirror be lowered in the bathroom so that when you look in it you cannot see your head, just the body.

"A few days of remembrance and you will feel such weightlessness happening to you, such tremendous silence, because it is the head that is the problem. If you can conceive of yourself as headless—and that can be conceived, there's no trouble in it—then more and more you will be centred in the heart.

"Just this very moment you can visualise yourself headless. Then you will understand what I mean immediately."

And the punch-line of the joke is that, following immediately on these exhortations to strenuous mind-work, is the solemn pronouncement "mind is rubbish"!

My reply is this. I don't think my head off, I see it off. I don't fantasise no head here, I find no head here, and in its place an immense Voidness. Non-violent, I don't behead myself (much less you) but cease denying that, for myself here, I terminate at shoulder level. This is honest and true seeing, taking in what's given, submitting to the evidence instead of mauling it.

(If you think I'm lying or fantasizing when I say I have no head here, you are invited to come all the way here and take a good look. I promise you that on the way to Me you will lose all trace of Harding.)

My second case is a well-known guru who saw himself as an anti-guru. His favourite topic was "the absence of the self", its ceasing to be, its giving place to the non-self. "We are all afraid of being nothing." But, he adds, "there is a state of action, a state of experiencing without the experiencer." It's our beliefs which cover up "the fear of being really nothing, of being really empty." And so on, in lecture after lecture after lecture, book after book. What (I ask) could be more true, more worth saying or more clearly said, more *meaningful*?

And more calculated to whet our appetite for the actual Experience?

Well, the following is part of a conversation, on October 9th, 1977, between this teacher (T) and one of his disciples (D)—or should I say long-time associates?

(D) I wondered if we could talk something over together. It's not a personal matter or a problem, but an aspect of perception I've been wanting to discuss with you for several years… It's to do with visual perception. You have often talked about visual perception, looking at a tree or a cloud, and so on, but mainly as a lead-in to talking about the structure of the mind.

(T) Yes.

(D) When I look at something, and observe the space between it and myself, then here (pointing at his own face), in that moment of attention, I find *nothing*: it is just emptiness.

(T) I don't understand those words "nothing" and "emptiness".

(D) I know that "nothing" is not a word to be used lightly.

(T) Then what do you mean by it, sir?

(D) I mean *absence,* the entire absence here (pointing to his face) of all the qualities perceived out there.

(T) But you can look in the mirror.

(D) It makes no difference. What is seen in the mirror is still absent on *this* side of the mirror.

(T) I haven't quite got it…. What does it mean in terms of action?

(D) I thought we could discuss whether it is true intrinsically.

(T) (Impatiently) I am not interested in intrinsically.

(D) It seems to me that one of the beauties of this insight is that it is always available.

(T) No, I can't accept that.

(D) It seems to me that even the simplest things take on a different significance when seen from this space.

(T) Not space. I won't accept that.

Equally famous and prolific is our third and last exponent of the Meaning without the Experience. He was interested, among many other things, in what I was up to, but didn't get it. On one occasion in the 70s, when he was staying with me in England, he hailed me at breakfast with the good news. At last he saw what I was on about. He had had a vivid dream in which everyone was headless!

Of course I did my best to explain to him that the headless or first-person Experience is essentially singular, and that second and third persons as such are by no means for beheading. But without effect, notwithstanding the fact that he was the most brilliant and versatile and popular Western writer of his generation on Zen and other spiritual disciplines. Or was his very brilliance the trouble?

Neither The Experience Nor The Meaning

On one hand I need hardly point out that most people are unprepared or unwilling to take the briefest peep into their Natureless Nature, let alone explore its wealth of implications and applications. Liberation is even rarer than sainthood. On the other hand I believe that the welfare of our species, and maybe its survival, depends on liberation becoming a great deal commoner (if not the norm by which maturity is judged) before it's too late.

However I must at once add that, unqualified, the rarity of liberation is a disastrous half-truth. The primary and saving whole truth is that we are all living from our Space and not our face, all doing it right, all firmly and forever established in our True Nature. To be at all is to be Being. In this sense all are awakened. The very fact that you and I don't fall over the furniture, that we take in these black-on-white printed patterns so effortlessly, is proof enough and to spare. Though the fact that we don't yet want to know this good news makes a huge practical difference, it makes no fundamental difference. In the last resort there's no other experience than this Experience. Only our Void Nature is Self-aware. All else is what It's aware of, Its Meaning.

Truly speaking, our Source has no Meaning whatever. In Itself It is infinitely beyond all that limited and limiting stuff, for nothing that can be said or thought or felt about It is It. Or let's put the matter like this: All right, the essential Experience of our Nature does have this most meaningful of Meanings—the Source of all meaning is Itself far beyond and absolutely free from all that proceeds from It. And You are One with That Source.

Conclusion

To end on a more mundane and practical note, let's ask which is the better way of beginning the Great Adventure? To go all out for the Meaning and risk missing the Experience, or to go all in for the Experience and risk missing the Meaning? To work *towards* awakening one day, or to work *from* it now? To practise with a view to seeing into our Void Nature eventually, or to practise the seeing from the start?

There is no "better way". It's instinct which settles which way we shall take—instinct which we go on to find good or bad reasons for, to justify as best we can.

My own instinct is no secret. My bank-balance being limited, I'll buy the horse of Experience before investing heavily in the cart of Meaning—at least I can get around on the animal. I choose to start with the engine rather than the chassis—at least I can run a dynamo off it to light my darkness.

Correction: "buy" is wrong. The Experience is gratis, with immediate free delivery of the whole package in a plain van. It's the Meaning that I have to buy on the never-never, unipart by unipart.

References

For the *Diamond Sutra,* on the fear of our Void Nature, see Edward Conze, *Buddhist Wisdom Books,* Allen and Unwin, London, 1958, p.53.

For "The Guillotine Meditation" see *The Orange Book: Meditation Techniques of Bhagwan Shree Rajneesh,* 1980, pp.75, 76.

For quotations from Krishnamurti see his *First and Last Freedom,* Gollancz, London, 1958, passim.

For an early and outstanding example of the work of Alan Watts see his *Way of Zen,* Thames and Hudson, London, 1957.

For Master Han Shan's observations on the two kinds of Zen yogis—those who begin with meaning and understanding, and those who begin with realisation—see Chang Chen-Chi, *The Practice of Zen,* Rider, London, 1959, pp.94, 95.

5. EYEBROWS UP!

Ray Cooney is a famous playwright and a producer and director of many West End shows, in which he has himself often appeared.

In the role of one of the tipsters in *Seize the Day, 366 Tips for Living (Chatto and Windus, 2001),* he writes: "As a comedy actor 'Eyebrows-Up' is the most helpful piece of advice that can be given. It is almost impossible to say a line incorrectly with your eyebrows up. It is also the way to go through life."

Ray Cooney knows what he's talking about. No matter how strange and dubious his recipe may seem, he has tested it so thoroughly and for so long that we dismiss it at our peril. At the very least he challenges us to ask WHY Eyebrows Up works so well for him and for the actors he has trained.

No doubt this question can be (and needs to be) addressed at several levels and from several points of view—physiological, psychological, sociological, and metaphysical. In this chapter I outline my own answer, leaving it to you to decide which of these levels my answer belongs to, and whether it does answer the question of WHY Eyebrows Up works so well.

Ray Cooney is talking about Eye Language, so let's begin with that subject. With a few random instances of the way we all use our eyes for sending silent messages to one another and for reinforcing spoken messages.

(1) At a gathering, recognising a friend in the distance, I signal "Hi!" to him or her by means of a pop-eyed stare. In other words, by raising my eyebrows. He or she responds by doing the same thing. (To tell the truth, not at all the same thing: I see those eyebrows go up and I feel these eyebrows go up.) This welcoming stare, this rounding of our eyes in all its variations, goes on unnoticed, but we are adepts at it.

(2) When I was about thirteen I took a mild dislike to one of my teachers (her name was Miss Blamey). I remember only one thing she ever said to me, and that was: "If looks could kill!" Evidently I had been looking at her with eyebrows down and eyes narrowed. If I had been looking at her with eyebrows up and eyes rounded it's unlikely she would have said something about looks that enliven, but I feel sure she would have felt something of the sort.

(3) Language itself is eloquent about the messages that pass between us without benefit of the spoken word. We "eye" and "make eyes at" one another, and some of us give a prospective sexual partner "the glad eye". To be in good form and lively is to be "bright-eyed and bushy-tailed". According to the old cliché, "the eyes are the windows of the soul". "Drink to me only with thine eyes," goes the well-loved song, "and I will pledge with mine".

(4) Why is the staring owl alone among birds (and even among creatures in general) popularly accredited with profound wisdom?

It's as if he were Ray Cooney's star pupil!

(5) Wise men philosophise, and the beginning and the end of philosophy is wonder, and wonder is notoriously not only wide-eyed but pop-eyed, or even goggle-eyed. So I say: Don't bother listening to a professional or amateur philosopher who addresses you with beetling brow. He is a beetle!

(6) In the *Tao Te Ching* and the *New Testament* we are advised that the wise thing to do is become like infants again. Have you ever been frowned upon or brow-beaten by a real baby? The cartoon sort do it all the time, of course.

(7) In practice there are countless variations on the pop-eyed stare. It may mean almost anything from "I find you contemptible!" to "Keep off!" to "You interest me strangely" to "I adore you!". And it's all done subliminally by means of a great variety of subtle adjustments

to the muscular tensions in and around the region of the eyes (what other part of the body is anything like so sensitive-expressive and so versatile?) while the more-or-less conscious act of Eyeing stays the same throughout. It's as if the Eye were the Great Communicator who's happy to leave to his wonderfully efficient staff the chore of composing and sending messages. It seems that the Cooney Recipe for Living consists of doing just one simple thing, which takes astonishingly good care of the innumerable unique and unforeseeable complexities that life is continually coming up with. We may be pretty sure that the actors he has trained are a lot better than the average citizen at communicating the nuances of human experience, and are certainly in no danger of becoming Cooney-clones or zombies or robots of any kind. Quite the contrary, in fact.

Here's a paradox, all right! As in the Japanese *NO* theatre, the star performer, because he or she is cool and poker-faced to the nth degree, expresses to perfection whatever feelings the dramatic occasion calls for!

Well, these random jottings are enough to confirm the importance (if confirmation were needed) of Ray Cooney's recipe for doing a good job on and off the stage. They will also serve as an introduction to my own reason for taking that recipe very seriously indeed, and my explanation of why it works so well.

As follows.

At once I note five immense advantages about this recipe for the good life.

1. It couldn't be easier for us humans to do.

2. It can't be done badly, it's always perfectly done.

3. It's done instantly.

4. And at will.

5. It is cleansed of spirituality and all that.

Admittedly, though Eyebrows Up is very strong as regards experience—the actual FEEL of it—it is altogether weak as regards meaning. But this weakness turns out to be a huge advantage, since it accounts for those five immense advantages.

As for myself, when I give Eyebrows Up a fair trial, I discover an astonishing thing. Which is this: the actual experience—I mean the FEEL I get from Eyebrows Up—is exactly the same as the FEEL I get from consciously looking out of my Single Eye, my God's Eye. In other words, for me the two experiences—Single Eye or Eyebrows Up - coincide.

So I ask myself: Why should I not substitute Eyebrows Up for Single Eye, which lacks all 5 advantages?

In particular, the Single Eye Experience

1. is arrived at by only a very limited number of people

2. is often done badly

3. takes time

4. isn't always done readily at will

5. reeks of spirituality and all that.

So I ask myself: Why should I not substitute for the Single Eye Experience—I mean the actual FEEL of it—the Eyebrows Up Experience, with its immense advantages?

The only reason I can think of is pride.

Of course I can point to the fact that the meaning arrived at by Cooney and Company is the production of West End shows. Yes, but I don't know what developments follow in their non-professional life from the practice. For all I know Eyebrows Up, in the private non-professional lives of Cooney and Company, may be giving rise to wonderful things. On a par with the meaning for me and friends of the Single Eye, which is to save all from pain and guilt.

Of course I am not proposing to give up the sharing and cultivation of the Single Eye. What I am proposing for myself (and some friends I hope) is substituting the moment-to-moment Eyebrows Up practice for the Single Eye practice.

6. NOTICE WHAT YOU SEE

In *Seize the Day, 366 Tips for living,* I also happen to have a tip (for February 12) for living. It runs like this:

NOTICE WHAT YOU SEE

When we dare to doubt what we are told and take a fresh look at what's going on, we are in for lots of pleasant and fascinating and useful surprises. A new and more satisfying way of life begins to open up, just by noticing what we see.

For instance, if you find the long journey to and from work tiring, just notice that it's the scenery that's doing all the rushing about, while you take a nice rest. If you find your eyes getting tired and tensions developing in that region, just notice that what you are looking out of is one huge and relaxed Eye, and not a pair of tiny screwed up peepholes in a box. If you feel ill at ease with some people, shy or often too self-conscious, just notice that what you are looking out of is not a face, but a huge and tranquil Space for taking in those faces. If you are scared of spiders, or the possibility of cancer, or of death, just notice that the Awake Space that you really are at centre is quite safe in all emergencies. This is a small sample of the welcome surprises that are there for the noticing.

7. SURELY HE HATH BORNE OUR GRIEFS

One of the most moving passages in the Old Testament is the prophet Isaiah's account of the Suffering Servant which, in the King James Version of the Bible, runs as follows:

Who hath believed our report, and to whom is the arm of the Lord revealed?

> For he shall grow up before Him as a tender plant, and as a root out of a dry ground; he hath no form or comeliness; and when we shall see him, there is no beauty that we should desire him.
>
> He is despised and rejected of men; a man of sorrows and acquainted with grief; and we hid as it were our faces from him.
>
> Surely he hath borne our griefs, and carried our sorrows; yet we did esteem him stricken, smitten of God, and afflicted.
>
> But he was wounded for our transgressions, he was bruised for our iniquities; the chastisement of our peace was upon him; and with his stripes we are healed.
>
> All we like sheep have gone astray; we have turned every one to his own way; and the Lord hath laid on him the iniquity of us all...

So far, the tale of the suffering Servant is apt to read like one of unrelieved misery and injustice, meted out by a barbarous Deity hungry for human sacrifice. But the much more cheerful sequel suggests that we may have to change our minds.

When Thou shall make his soul an offering for sin, he shall see his seed, he shall prolong his days, and the pleasure of the Lord shall prosper in his hand.

He shall see of the travail of his soul, and shall be satisfied.

It seems that Jesus of Nazareth was familiar with this important Old Testament text, and deliberately modeled his life and his dying on it. Certainly Christians down the centuries have believed that it foretold the story of their beloved redeemer, who suffered and died for them all. They have followed the lead of the gospel-maker Matthew, who announced that Jesus suffered "that it might be fulfilled which was spoken by Isaiah the prophet, saying: Himself took on our infirmities and bare our sicknesses." And there is no doubt that Saint Paul, the architect of Christianity, deliberately took on the Redeemer's role, declaring "I am crucified with Christ, nevertheless I live: yet not I, but Christ liveth in me."

I am not asking you to believe that this strange story of vicarious suffering is a true story or to endorse it, but instead to look briefly with me into the reason for its hold on so many for so long. In other words to uncover what truth (if any) underlies it. If you happen to be a believing Christian, I am asking you to heed the warning of a great Christian—Saint Bernard of Clairvaux—"In darkness we abide so long as we walk in belief and not in beholding." Throughout this enquiry I would like us all to take that warning very seriously indeed, *and for a change to test what we are told by what we behold instead of vice versa.*

I am addressing the problem of pain. And in particular the problem of the body that suffers pain—what and whose it is, and how it differs from a body that doesn't suffer pain. And because I am literally in no position here to speak for you I shall speak for myself alone, leaving it to you to check whether what's true for me where I am happens to be true for you where you are. All the same, I shall be delighted if we can get together and see eye to eye in this life-or-death matter.

I sport *two* bodies, and can't do with less. Though intimately connected and both human, they are usually upwards of a metre apart. As well as very different in all sorts of ways. Here's a sketch of what they look like to me:

Let's call these bodies No.1 and No.2. Among their more striking difference I behold the following—

No.1 belongs on this, the near side of my mirror, while No.2 belongs on that, the far side of my mirror. Or, as we normally put it, in my mirror.

No.1 has (or should I say is?) a single boundless Eye, while No.2 has two small eyes in a head.

The spread arms of No.1 easily embrace as much of the wide world as happens to be on offer, while those of No.2 embrace only a small part of that world.

The feel of No.1 is rough and irregular and ticklish and rather warm, while the feel of No.2 is shiny-smooth and regular and not at all ticklish and rather cool.

No.1 is bigger than No.2 and stays roughly the same size, whereas No.2 is elastic. Sometimes it's very tiny.

No.1 is anonymous, a What's-his-name lacking a particular human identity, whereas No.2 has all the marks of Douglas Harding to the exclusion of all others.

No.1 looks all around and at others as he pleases, whereas No.2 has the curious habit of fixedly staring at No.1. It's as if courtly etiquette requires him to acknowledge No.1's majesty by never turning his back on him.

Though in fact there are (all dutifully lined up for beholding) innumerable differences between my two bodies, this short list will do for the present. But not even the most striking of these differences should be allowed to diminish the necessity and importance of *both* of them, or their profound interdependence. Thanks to those differences they dovetail perfectly. Thus No.1 has only to wiggle a finger for No.2 to follow suit immediately; thus it takes the two of them to reveal whether there's egg on one's beard; thus the big job of No.2 is to provide No.1 with the handiest and vividest demonstration of what he's not like. The truth is that No.1 has just as much need of No.2's Hardingness as of its own freedom from Hardingness.

This leaves me with three crucial questions to be asked and answered (by beholding, of course) about these two bodies of mine.

(i) Where am I?

To need and have two bodies doesn't mean that I inhabit both in the same manner and at the same time and for the same purposes. Not at all! Though it's true we currently share the same address and telephone number, there are times when I locate myself in and feel at home in No.1, and other times when I locate myself in and feel at home in No.2. Actually I *commute,* day in and day out, hourly, all the blessed time, between them.

This unremitting to-and-fro does not mean, however, that I'm equally comfy and wide-awake in either of them, as if one were my fine town house and the other were my charming country cottage. Not a bit of it! When I'm abiding in No.1 I'm quite sure that this is where I belong, this is Home Ground, this is WHERE I AM WHAT I AM, and in all other places it seems I'm pretending to be what I'm not. No wonder that, when I find myself lurking in No.2, the self I find there has a vague and uneasy feeling that it's a displaced person.

(ii) When am I?

HERE's now and THERE's then. To inhabit body No.2 is to keep mulling over the past and future (to little or no effect) in a vain attempt to be when I'm not. Whereas to inhabit body No.1 is to catch up with myself and get down to the immediate business of living. Here and now is where I literally come to my senses and experience the tang and tingle and thrill of life. Apparently No.1 is my real and ever-present body, while No.2 is my not-so-real and ever-absent body. Let me put it like this. No.2 was and shall be but never is, while No.1 never was and never shall be but always is, and so between them both (it seems) Time's wrapped up rather neatly. Of this I'm sure— life consciously lived in the present moment is life transformed, life enlivened.

(iii) What am I?

What is this mysterious What's-his-name? What am I where and when I really, really am, in body No.1? Among all possible answers to this most searching of questions, one stands out. It is that I am ONE-OFF, UNIQUE, ALONE. You could say that I'm a species so endangered that it's reduced to a single specimen—provided you added that, as it turns out, I'm the only species that isn't endangered! Not once in the 93 years of my human life have I glimpsed another body No.1, and I have every reason to suppose it's nowhere to be found. If I re-christen myself *this first person,* this first person is always *first person singular.*

Let me remind you and myself that I'm taking Saint Bernard's tip very seriously, and backing what I behold instead of what I'm told. I'm putting my shirt on what I see I see instead of what I fancy I see.

The results are, to say the least, as startling as they are painful. Body No.1 (which is visibly alone, one of one) suffers pain; while body No.2 (which is visibly one of many) suffers no pain. This can only mean that I TAKE ON THE PAIN OF THE WORLD! And the old Jewish prophet's story of the Suffering Servant turns out to be the truest and most up-to-date and gripping—and awful, and awe-inspiring—of stories. It *hurts* to be incarnated this side of my looking-glass.

I know of no other cure for unhappiness than this most drastic and truly homeopathic cure—namely: more, much more of the same. Not up and away from grief (what a hope!) but down and into and through. That's the way. Go for the world's happiness and be happy; go for your own happiness and be miserable.

But just a minute! Two powerful objections crop up here. First, my pain (thank God!) falls immeasurably short of the world's pain, and its midsummer madness to suppose I'm taking on the lot. And second, the same must be said of my joy—which (to say the least) is as imperfect as it's intermittent.

The reason for this double shortfall could be one or more of the following. (i) To some degree I'm *repressing* the pain, and it's time I ceased to do so. And the same is true of the pleasure. (ii) It's early days. The pain has to be worked through, and lived through, and this takes time. Wait for it! Joy cometh in the morning. (iii) I need to recognize that God in His mercy reduces both pain and its opposite to manageable proportions, to what One Person can bear. The suffering of a thousand people isn't a thousand times more severe than the suffering of just one of them. Neither pain nor pleasure adds up that way, and ordinary arithmetic doesn't apply here. Though not even He can create joy without pain (any more than He can create left without right or up without down), He can and He does limit vicarious suffering without limiting its healing power.

At this point I have to confess that, in spite of all the piled-up evidence that the One I really am takes on the world's pain, there are times when I forget it. Surely (I say to myself) the suffering is built in and universal and horribly cruel, and every creature is stuck with its own share of it.

Well, that's undoubtedly the case at one level. But there are other levels. The real is relative, a marvelous multi-level magic. At one level, for instance, I'm Nothing, at another a United Cellular Republic (very much more populous than the USA), at another a Man, at another a Cosmos—all depends on the range of my observer. When you come to me bearing gifts—with a contribution, an opinion, an objection—I don't ask myself *whether* it's valid, but *at what level* it's valid. I have become convinced that there is a Place and a Level at which every creature is relieved of suffering. My main reason for this conviction follows presently.

Meantime a further objection insists on coming up. Let's put it this way:

This primitive obsession with human sacrifice (insufficiently up-graded and ennobled and sanctified by dubbing it vicarious suffering) is the speciality of Western religion, and in particular of Judeo-Christianity, whereas the best Eastern religions are comparatively free of it. Can we afford to ignore their view of these matters?

To which I answer: Each major religion, Eastern or Western, has its own unique way of accounting for and putting into practice what we call vicarious suffering. Let's take, for instance, Buddhism, which teaches that wisdom or enlightenment without compassion is unwise and endarkening and won't do at all. The word compassion (coming from the Latin) means *suffering with,* and the dedicated Buddhist deliberately suffers with *all* beings. Not content with subjective feelings of universal compassion and love, he sends these feelings out in one direction after another (it's a kind of super-radar, so to say) till the pain of every creature in the cosmos is taken care of.

It wasn't more than ten minutes after writing the preceding paragraph that I happened to notice, on the bookshelves of my Los Angeles hostess Virginia, a book entitled *Only Don't Know,* by the Korean Zen Master Seung Sahn[1]. Imagine my excitement when, casually thumbing through its pages, I discovered that it consists of correspondence between the Master and his student-disciples, *each letter of spiritual counsel ending with the Master's fervent hope that he or she will go on to SAVE ALL BEINGS FROM SUFFERING!* Here Seung Sahn lines up with *The Diamond Sutra* of Mahayana Buddhism, in which we read: "All Bodhisattvas should discipline

---

1 *Only Don't Know,* Selected Teaching Letters of Zen Master Seung Sahn, Shambhala, Boston and London.

their thoughts as follows: I enable all living beings to Unbounded Liberation, Nirvana."

In fact, every Bodhisattva solemnly vows to save all sentient beings. D. T. Suzuki, who brought Zen to the West, writes, "It is the heart indeed that tells us that our own self is a self only to the extent that it disappears into all other selves, non-sentient as well as sentient." Which brings us back to the Buddha's own enlightenment. According to Theravada tradition, his enlightenment was none other than the enlightenment of all sentient beings, past and present and future. Though it may seem a fantastic story, I have come to see it as a true story and the pattern of all real enlightenment. You could say it's a Buddhist realisation, though not uniquely so.

It is much less evident in Hinduism and Advaita-Vedanta. Vivekananda, however, does come up with: "Each is responsible for the evil anywhere in the world." As for Christianity, this total transformation of individual salvation into universal salvation seems more at home in the Eastern Orthodox Church than in Western Catholicism. Thus Nicolai Berdayev: "All must be saved and liberated from hell. This is the last and final demand of ethics. Direct all the power of your spirit to freeing everyone from hell." And John of Cronstadt, who was a parish priest, says: "When you pray, endeavour to pray more for others than for yourself alone, and during prayer represent to yourself vividly all men as forming one body with yourself... Look upon their infirmities and sickness as your own, their spiritual ignorance, their sins and passions as your own."

Here in the West, however, we do find some echoes of this radical and revolutionary teaching. Flannery O'Connor, an American novelist, says of one of his characters: "He saw that no sin was too monstrous to claim as his own." And there is Richard Jefferies who writes: "From every human being whose body has been racked by pain, from every human being who has suffered from accident or disease, from every human being drowned, burned, or slain by negligence, there goes up a continuously increasing cry louder than the thunder... These miseries are your doing."

It is Antoine de Saint Exupéry who writes: "In the hands of each rests the salvation of all."

But it's to Edwin Muir, the Scottish poet that I now turn with special happiness and admiration. For me he announces and celebrates the doctrine that the Buddha's enlightenment was the enlightenment and salvation not only of present and future souls but also of all past souls and the undoing of the world's terrible history.

Then he will come, Christ the uncrucified,
Christ the discrucified, his death undone,
His agony unmade, his cross dismantled –
Glad to be so—and the tormented wood
Will cure its hurt and grow into a tree
In a green springing corner of young Eden,
And Judas damned take his long journey backward
From darkness into light and be a child
Beside his mother's knee, and the betrayal
Be quite undone and never more be done.

These lines are part of Muir's poem *The Transfiguration*. They put perfectly what happens when Time and the Salvation of the World get together.

Let me explain.

Time's the trouble. And yes, I know I have often said—and for sure will go on saying—that the way is *down and into the things of time, not up and away from them.*

Yes, but down and into things of time happens to be down and into the timeless Centre of all of us sentient beings. Here at Centre we are rid of Time, totally shot of Time and all its works.

"Rejoice in God all the time", says St. Paul. "He rejoices all the time who rejoices beyond time and free from time", adds Eckhart.

But alas the great majority of Christians suffer from an idolatrous obsession with events and things in time.

I must remind you and myself here that Timelessness and Salvation don't come on the cheap. I have deliberately to take on all that past suffering if I am to take it away.

In general, we may safely say that all real spirituality has its own version of vicarious suffering and of Isaiah's Suffering Servant.

But the trouble with taking on all this misery is that I'm overwhelmed, sunk far below the surface where blows God's wind and shines the clear air of God's joy.

Dom John Chapman (1865-1933) who was the Fourth Abbott of Downside, and a very gifted and respected director of souls, confirms one's misery. Here is a typical piece of advice to one of his correspondents: "Say to yourself 'I have nothing; I am useless; I am simply a lump of wretchedness'. This is a kind of worry or anxiety, but it is *the only way* of having peace with God." In the latter part of his life he was much influenced by Jean Pierre de Caussade, S.J. (1675-1751) who was the spiritual director of a number of highly educated and devoted nuns. One after another these pious women wrote to him telling their tragic story, to the effect that when they took the veil they were full of love and joy and trust in God, but now, after a lapse of a few years of the religious life, they had lost it all. They were desperately wretched and even subject to doubts about God and the Christian faith. True, they went on living the life of a dedicated religious out of habit, notwithstanding its misery. He was so happy for them, and thoroughly delighted with their report. This was the true spiritual life at last. Now they were in it for the truth and for real, and no longer for the pleasant feelings that it brought at the start.

Yes, but there was another and very different side to De Caussade. He was the author of a collection of teachings entitled *The Sacrament of the Present Moment,* in which he says "God is telling you, dear sisters, that if you abandon all restraint, carry your wishes to their furthest limits, open your hearts boundlessly, there is not a single moment when you will not be shown everything you can possibly wish for. The present moment holds infinite riches beyond your wildest dreams."

Divine bliss is nearer to me than my human misery, and it's impossible to exaggerate my spendour or yours at heart. In fact we would do well to heed here the warning of St. Francis of Sales that the Evil One is pleased with sadness and melancholy. A Hassid Rabbi writes: "It is good if man can bring about that God sings within him." Another Rabbi points out that "all joys hail from Paradise".

O He gives to us His joy
That our grief He may destroy,

says William Blake, and Lady Julian of Norwich, along with others of similar spiritual stature, tells us that all our goodness and love and joy are really those of the Indwelling God, and therefore in the long run all is very well indeed.

Of course I don't know about you, but this hugely uplifting message, coming to me from such diverse and widely-scattered and impressive quarters, is very encouraging, but not so easy to put into daily practice. I have to admit that while Man's misery comes easily to me, God's joy is not so forthcoming. In fact it's often damned difficult, and impossible, to take on board. Though I'm deeply convinced of the facts, my feelings are slow to follow suit.

What can I do?

Only this. I can and I must and I do say to the God who is much more me than I am me: "It takes You, with all your divine bliss and splendor, to be God in me—a task which is utterly, utterly beyond my human comprehension and contriving. Dear Lord, I'm handing the job over to You. You *are* my joy unbounded. Deal it out to me in your own time and way. That time and way must be the best both for the world which You have given me to save, and for me "personally".

And then, I have to say, there does descend on me the peace that passes understanding. This is His peace. In the last resort it is inseparable from and none other than His joy.

Shankara who is the very great (if not the greatest) Hindu sage and philosopher, in his *Commentaries on the Brihadaranyaka Upanishad* (edited by A. J. Alston, Shanti Sadan, 1987, p.68) writes:

"This 'being-the-Self-of-all' is the highest state of consciousness of the Self, His supreme natural state. But when, before this, one feels oneself to be other than the Self of all, even by a hair's breadth, that state is nescience, avidya, delusion."

8. MISS SMITH GOES TO HELL

Miss Smith complains: I don't know how long I've been stuck in this dreadful place, but it seems ages. I wonder if God in heaven can hear the cries of us wretched creatures in hell.

Lord God: Yes, very clearly.

Miss Smith: Is that really You?

L.G.: Yes.

M.S.: Good Heavens! This is astonishing!... Do you know just how awful it is down here?

L.G.: Well, I'd like to hear all about it from you. Please tell Me exactly what's the trouble.

M.S.: It's all trouble, and trouble's far too mild a word for it.

L.G.: I'm listening.

M.S.: I don't know where to begin.

L.G.: Why not with the worst of it?

M.S.: I think the worst of it is what I might call my spiritual degeneration, the collapse and disappearance—or what's more horrible, the reversal—of all the spiritual progress I thought I had made. Twenty years ago I went through the motions of dedicating my life to you. Conscious union with my Source was my aim, and for a few months, or let's say a year or so, I really felt from time to time that I was achieving this lofty aim. In fact I experienced so much joyous satisfaction (or should I say joyous self-satisfaction?) that I couldn't help trying to share it with anyone who would give me a hearing.

L.G.: Then what happened?

M.S.: I blush to say that I burgeoned into some kind of teacher, a very minor spiritual authority, and soon acquired a following. And then...

L.G.: Then what happened?

M.S.: I discovered I was a fraud!

L.G.: You don't think that's putting it rather strongly?

M.S.: Not in my case. All that spiritual progress, my Lord, proved to be illusory, seeing that it so soon gave rise to wretchedness instead of joy. Was this a morass of misery that I was busy leading my disciples into? I asked myself. Could I be doing them a more cruel disservice? Every day and in every way I was getting worse and doing more harm.

L.G.: Are you really as awful as all that?

M.S.: Worse.

L.G.: What about your clear seeing into your No-thingness at Centre, into your Void Nature? Has it, too, forsaken you? Have you gone blind to what you used to say was clearer, and simpler, and much more obvious than anything else?

M.S.: No, Lord. But instead of triggering peace and joy it triggers their opposites. Which can only mean that something's gone radically wrong with my seeing. Something I'll never fathom.

L.G.: Are you sure that very special vision can go wrong?

M.S.: Practically sure, Lord.

L.G.: How can No-thingness go wrong if there's nothing in it to go wrong?

M.S.: With God all things are possible, they tell me!

L.G.: Well, we'll see. Be prepared to change your mind. Meantime please tell Me the rest of what's troubling you.

M.S.: It's bad enough being a lost soul and a hopeless case oneself, but to be this in an equally helpless world is too much, if You'll allow me to say so. Once upon a time I used to enjoy seasons of mild optimism, when I felt that, thanks to You, the whole frightening story would come right in the end. But now my own dreadful state and the world's dovetail so neatly that there remains no escape, no glimmer of hope.

L.G.: Have you told me all your worries? What else is troubling you?

M.S.: As if that lot weren't enough!

L.G.: Come on Miss Smith! I want you to off-load all your suffering onto Me. Tell Me the rest. Are you in dreadful pain?

M.S.: Just now I wouldn't put it quite like that. It's more like an unrelieved feeling of anxiety and self-disgust and despair. Here am I stuck in hell, and thoroughly deserving to stay stuck here for all time and eternity. Sometimes I figure that the worst thing of all is that You are, for the best of reasons, utterly fed up and finished with me, and I deserve nothing but your loathing and contempt. You must be as appalled as I am at this morass I call my mind. Nowadays it seems incapable of a cheerful, generous, true idea, but instead is full to overflowing with oceans of garbage, most of it stinking garbage, at that. And instead of getting better I'm getting nastier every day, as You well know.

L.G.: So you haven't a good word to say for yourself.

M.S.: Not one, O Lord. Moreover, I confess, hardly a good word to say for You. Even the word God has come to mean almost nothing to me. I'm a spiritual disaster, if ever there was one.

L.G.: Well, thank you very much, Miss Smith, for unburdening yourself so frankly. I'm taking your word for it that you have no confidence whatever left in yourself, in your own merits and resources.

M.S.: You know very well, Lord, that all the stuffing has been knocked out of me, that nothing's left but failure, wretchedness and disgust.

L.G.: Well, Miss Smith, are you sure you've finished?

M.S.: No. The most horrible thing about these horrors is that there's no end to them. Hell's for ever.

L.G.: Hold on a minute! Brace yourself for the shock of your life! I have news for you, Miss Smith, wonderful news!

M.S.: I can't wait for it.

L.G.: Though in a sense I agree you have been telling Me the truth, and I would be very sorry if you were to change your mind about yourself and go back to your early spiritual bumptiousness, in a deeper sense you've got things all upside-down. I have to tell you that what you see as spiritual degeneration is really spiritual maturing. A very rare and special blessing has been poured out on you, Miss Smith. Let Me put it like this. The price of Union with Me is disunion with yourself, and the awful story you have just told Me is in fact the best of all stories. To want absolutely all of Me is to want absolutely none of you, and to get it in spades. There's no other doorway to our joint bliss. Your seemingly sad tale gives Me great joy, a joy that I long to share to the full with you. I do assure you that your experience down here in hell is at once my precious and indispensable gift to you and yours to Me. With all my heart I thank you.

M.S.: This is incredible! Not content with banishing me for ever to this chamber of horrors, I now find You peeping in at the door, mocking me.

L.G.: So far from mocking you I'm telling you that I need you as much as you need Me. And there's no other way of satisfying both of us but this way. Your early illusion of spiritual progress, though excusable, was very dangerous, and I admit I did what I could to polish it off.

M.S.: You sent me to hell!

L.G.: I wouldn't put it like that.

M.S.: And now You are going to hoist me out of it?

L.G.: Again, I wouldn't put it like that.

M.S.: If that isn't mocking me, what is?

L.G.: If here's the only place where You and I are One—and in a true sense it is—are you quite sure you still want to escape from it?

M.S.: Of course not, Lord, provided I were absolutely sure of our Oneness. Do You really think it's possible to stay perfectly certain of it down here?

L.G.: Here's where you give up on yourself, and here's where I give up on Myself, and as a consequence we are perfectly united. This is Love indeed.

M.S.: I hear You describing heaven, not hell.

L.G.: These are words. Let's go back to exactly what you are looking out of right now. How would you describe it, Miss Smith?

M.S.: As unbounded, wide-awake Clarity. As Emptiness or Nothing for filling with Everything. As Space for the world to happen in. As Capacity Itself. As…

L.G.: Cross my heart, you are also describing Me. Which can only mean that we are looking out of exactly the same Clarity. Which can only mean that you and I are One. Now tell Me, Miss Smith, do you still want to get out of here at the earliest possible opportunity?

M.S.: Or, instead, should I re-christen this place, calling it by a very different name? Being surely and for ever oned with You, Lord, it should be easy to stick it out here, or anywhere else. But I know I'll fail miserably without your constant help.

L.G.: Which you have, I promise you.

M.S.: One other thing. Forgive me for asking, Lord, why You, who are omnipotent, saw fit to fix up our union by consigning me, along with so many others, to hell? Surely You could have settled on a kinder way?

L.G.: If I could have done so, I would have done so. But I assure you that, because in the last resort you and I are One and the Same for ever and ever, I have been feeling as and for you all along. To neither of us does our union come cheap. But at this point I'd like to check exactly where we stand by asking you a few more questions.

M.S.: Fire away!

L.G.: The first is this. Will you believe Me when I assure you that I've made my home at your very Centre?

M.S.: Well for years I believed it and talked about it, and if now You reassure me, then my answer is Yes.

L.G.: Do you agree, then, that you should be radiant with my bliss, but are not?

M.S.: That's precisely my trouble.

L.G.: Now which of us wants it to be like that, you or Me?

M.S.: Not me, I swear.

L.G.: And certainly not Me... Well, how shall we unblock this log-jam?

M.S.: At least You have some suggestions to make.

L.G.: It could help if you were to ask yourself which of us, though by far the more powerful, is the more reluctant to impose his or her will upon the other.

M.S.: I think I'm getting your point, Lord, to the effect that it's I who have opted for hell and misery, and that if I were to let You have your way, I would be radiant with your heavenly bliss.

L.G.: Well, what have you to lose by inviting Me to have my way with you, and seeing what happens?

9. A 1972 WORKSHOP

At the 1972 Buddhist Summer School a group of around twenty people met daily for about two hours, not to listen to a lecture, not to discuss any topic, not to meditate, but to take part in an activity called a workshop. This article outlines the purpose, the principles, the procedure, and the results of such a workshop.

Purpose

The purpose of the workshop is that each member shall turn his attention to what he is in his own experience, to how it always is where he is. To what it's like being first-person singular present tense. This is *not* a psychological investigation into the ever-changing patterns of his thoughts and feelings, but bare attention to the constant background of these patterns. In other words, the aim is that he shall see into what the Buddhists call his changeless original nature.

Principles

The basic idea of the workshop is that we don't learn by what we read or are told by others, or even by what we ourselves think or feel, but by what we discover in action. Real learning is doing, trying things out. And it is easier to try things out in a group than individually (1) because most of the useful experiments involve other people anyway, (2) because members of the group help each other and make joint discoveries, (3) because it is much easier to concentrate for an hour or so in a group than on one's own, and (4) because it is more fun.

In a workshop everyone participates and anything may happen (the leader's job is not to impose a programme, but to keep people from straying too far from the point); so it is alive, and no-one is likely to fall asleep. And, if the workshop works, no-one goes out of it unchanged.

Procedure

Over the past three years a repertoire of exercises and games and experiments—aids to seeing into one's original nature—has been developed. Since they are all designed to this one end, it isn't necessary to work through them all: any one of them is sufficient to make the point. On the other hand, a large and varied repertoire is useful because people are so very unlike and my way isn't necessarily yours: different temperaments are catered for. Moreover each way confirms and reinforces the others. To come to the one central experience from several directions doesn't add to that experience, but does underline its accessibility, leaving us with no excuse for avoiding any longer the fundamental truth about ourselves.

Two examples will make clear the sort of thing that goes on in the workshop.

Example: The Unclassifiable

A coloured sticker—red or green or blue or yellow—is stuck on the forehead of each participant by the workshop leader, who tells him to close his eyes while the sticker is put on. He is forbidden to look in a mirror, or ask others what his colour is, or tell them what theirs is. The group is then instructed to sort itself out into four sub-groups—all the reds in one, all the greens in another and so on—and to accomplish this sorting people may behave as they please, subject only to the rules already mentioned. What usually happens is that some wander around futilely trying to guess their colour, while others, completely baffled, just give up; till someone has a bright idea, and then the four sub-groups take shape in a few moments and everyone is duly classified.

The threefold lesson of this game is that, in and for oneself, one is forever absolutely unclassifiable, unlimited, no-thing, empty; that one contains all groups without belonging to any; and that one is classified and put into a group by *others,* for whom one is indeed a limited thing. One may read and re-read the sutras that say that one's original nature is like space, one may be told again and again that intrinsically one is qualityless, one may sincerely think and believe that this is so, one may in meditation feel (for a time) quite empty. But now at last the penny drops, as one stands there utterly vacant in the workshop, waiting to be taken in and made something of by one of the groups. Now there is no escape from one's voidness: one vividly *sees* what one is and isn't, *and this seeing is believing.*

Example: Onion-peeling

A workshop member, A, raises an objection. 'All right, so far. I see I'm nothing here *to myself.* But this could be a subjective illusion. Also relevant is what I appear to be *to others.* Why shouldn't I go by B's impression of me?'

Accordingly we go into the question of how A strikes B. A sits at one end of the room while B, standing at the opposite end, looks at him through a 'view-finder'—a sheet of paper with a small hole in it. B announces that the view here—say at twenty feet—is of a man. But there are other views to be had, other appearances to be explored. As he approaches A, slowly crossing the room, B's story changes radically. At, say, 10 feet, he finds a torso, then a head, then an eye, and finally—at almost no distance—there is a mere blur in his view-finder. He explains that what he is now experiencing is no longer a recognisable person, no longer anything classifiable: all this was left behind as he closed in. Now it is this remaining blur—or A himself—that must take up and complete B's tale, and tell its inside story. The blur declares that, to itself, it is nothing at all: A is empty of A. And this is precisely the conclusion that B's tale prepares us for. The outsider's views dovetail perfectly with the insider's.

But why (we may ask) go to the trouble of enacting on the workshop floor what should be plain enough already—the fact that by going right up to anything one loses it and approaches its central void?

A participant in a recent workshop answers the question: "For three years or more this idea—the notion that a 'thing' is a nest of appearances surrounding a central reality which is void—had been familiar and indeed obvious to me. I believed I had fully grasped it, and all the more so because my job was to work an electron microscope in a biological laboratory. Nevertheless it was only when, in a workshop, I actually took part in an 'onion-peeling exercise' that the meaning came home to me."

These two random examples of the many exercises (a number of which explore senses other than vision) are enough to illustrate the sort of thing that goes on in a workshop.

Results

Experience in North America, England, and on the Continent over the past two years, conducting workshops lasting for an hour or two to eight days, shows that any interested participant will realise the workshop's purpose and see (however briefly and intermittently) into his void nature. What he will then do with his in-seeing, whether he will go on with it till it becomes quite steady and natural and therefore fully operative, is of course another question. Certainly glimpsing the basic truth about himself can do him no harm, and even if he doesn't practise it at all he will not altogether lose the knack of in-seeing. Sooner or later he may find that he needs, above all things, to reactivate his own, first-hand workshop discoveries.

10. THE HEADLESS WAY IN 1965

Rummaging through some old papers in 2003, I found this long-forgotten essay. The version of *On Having No Head* it refers to is the original, published by the London Buddhist Society in 1961.

It is now about five years since *On Having No Head* was written. Up to then, I had met only one other person who I was sure had "lost her head". Between then and now, there have been a further nine cases (making eleven in all) known to me, most of them intimately. The purpose of these Notes is to draw some general conclusions from these additional cases.

1. What the experience is

The experience consists in *seeing* the non-existence of that part of one's body which happens for the moment to be invisible. This invisible part is at least one's head, but it is more often one's trunk or one's whole body (depending on whether one is looking down or ahead): in fact, it is as much of the universe as is right here, this side of one's spectacles. One sees that this is not merely invisible, but totally dissolved, gone without trace. It isn't a case of "I can't see my face" but "I see I have no face", which is a very different matter. This is the essential jump. It is not an intellectual leap, not an understanding of one's voidness. It is actually seeing the absolute clarity, the no-head here, and seeing it with the same sharpness as one sees the head over there in the mirror where it belongs, five feet from here.

2. Who it happens to

So far, in all but one instance, it has happened to men. The youngest was 16, the oldest 60, and the average age around 30. The intelligence was above average, and the personality fairly normal and stable. Apparently it is unlikely to happen to the mentally disturbed or the neurotic.

It has little connection with intellectual or moral or (manifest) spiritual maturity. It can happen at the very beginning of one's spiritual life, almost effortlessly, with hardly any previous search or discipline; or it can come only after many years of sustained effort. It is possible to spend a lifetime dedicated to the quest for self-knowledge, and achieve a controlled mind and much saintliness, without ever seeing.

3. How it happens

It happens by personal contact. So far as is known, only in one case has the book shown anyone his headlessness, and then the results have been reported as very meagre. At best, the book prepares for seeing, and confirms afterwards.

4. Its main characteristics

It is *sudden,* because it is all-or-nothing. Either it is seen or not seen; there is no intermediate state.

It is *definite,* not vague. One who sees cannot doubt the validity of what he sees, or his ability to see it. Nor can he confuse this experience with any other.

It is *surprising*, quite revolutionary, not a somewhat different way of looking at oneself.

Yet it is *unspectacular*, cool, not at all strange or pious or even religious, but entirely natural. It has nothing to do with ecstasy, flashes of light, or any abnormal states of mind. This is not a special or holy or spiritual sort of seeing: one sees the absence of one's head as one sees the absence of one's hand at point A, when it is moved to point B.

It is *obvious*, so blazingly obvious that one's initial reaction is likely to be laughter, and refusal to believe that anybody could fail to see this, once it was pointed out.

It is *always the same*, always total, incapable of improvement or decay. Yet it is never the same. Unchanging in its essence, it is infinitely varied in its expression. Every time is the first time: there is no carry-over from the past, no memory in the ordinary sense. The savour of seeing, though unmistakable, is subtly different on each occasion.

It is *recallable* at will. One can check one's absence whenever one wants to. Of course there are apt to be times when one is agitated or diverted, and therefore doesn't want to.

Above all, it is *discovery* of the basic truth about oneself, as it has always been. It is not an achievement or a possession.

5. Its main conditions

The body relaxed. It gradually becomes apparent to the seer that a distinctive kind of letting-go accompanies seeing. The whole body—

particularly the neck, shoulders, arms and hands, are deeply relaxed. Yet there develops a sensation of intensity, poise, inner power, an alertness pervading the entire organism. One is very still and easy, but more wide awake than usual.

The breathing slow. The out-breathing gets deeper, as if one were pressing down the diaphragm, and the rate of breathing becomes very slow. In the end the breathing is hardly perceptible. All this happens without any conscious interference.

The mind empty. Seeing is a state of not thinking, without memory, anticipation, intention, ideas, words. It is bare Consciousness aware of Itself as such. (Yet, paradoxically, it can be enjoyed while speaking, listening, thinking.)

The feelings at rest. It is a state of tranquillity, untroubled by any kind of emotion.

6. Its secondary effects

These vary somewhat from individual to individual. Not everyone experiences them all in full measure—or at any rate not to begin with.

Colour and pattern. Colours are miraculously brilliant: they shine and glow as never before. The colour combinations and shadings, the patterns and textures of things, their movements—all are observed to be very beautiful, precious, profoundly inevitable. The ordinary world is actually perceived at last, and turns out to be heaven itself. Oddly enough, this is because one isn't looking at it, but rather at the one who is looking.

Music. One's taste in music, as in all the arts, is altered. It is no longer conventional, but genuine, and so holds many surprises. Those who see have, for instance, a tendency to pick the same pieces or phrases (ranging from pop and folk to the classics) because they have an extraordinary power of expressing the joy and energy and mystery of This which sees and is seen.

Ordinary life. Natural functions and sensations—relieving one's bowels, eating and drinking, walking, bathing, resting, and so on—all are now so savoured that one is never bored. The simplest things, their scents and feel and the noises they make, are full of new interest. Best of all is the pleasure of just being.

Efficiency. One can now concentrate. The result is that one's work gets done much faster and better than before. It's as though it does itself without one's conscious intervention.

Getting on with people. One's relationships are much eased. Shyness and awkwardness and hostility give way to spontaneous and natural and kindly behaviour.

Seeing people as they are. One no longer judges conventionally, from snobbish or self-seeking motives, but sees faults as faults and virtues as virtues. One is much more perceptive and less likely to be taken in. Yet there is no feeling of superiority to anyone. Or of inferiority, for that matter.

Happiness. Moods tend to even out. Anxiety, fear, and depression gradually become as impossible as being in love, or hating anyone. By and large, and in spite of constant and often severe tests and trials, this is the life of true happiness. But it takes time to settle down.

The initial surprise and joy of seeing are apt to be followed by a period of dryness or loneliness, or depression of some kind. This phase will pass more quickly if one realises what it is—a deepening and consolidation, to be followed by a state of steady tranquillity.

Meditation. Seeing is found to be more or less independent of time and place and posture. It can be at its most vivid in a crowded street. Meditational techniques become largely irrelevant, as does most of the machinery of religion. The only meditation for the headless one is headlessness—the Absence, the Clarity here alive to Itself. If he tries to keep up his meditation on set topics, or meditation with any content at all, he is likely to find he cannot do so.

7. How deep and permanent is this seeing?

When there has been no previous spiritual search, no strong desire to find the Truth about oneself, can seeing occur? It certainly can. But the chances are that it will be undervalued, and perhaps not followed up at all. To be effective, it must be wanted, and its spiritual significance grasped. Can one who has clearly seen, who has for months and years earnestly extended his seeing till he sees much of the time—can such a one fall away and revert to the old life of blindness? Indeed he can, and very quickly indeed. Seeing certainly weakens the ego, by undermining its very basis. But the ego's destruction is a very long and hard business: it puts up an obstinate and subtle fight, and can be quite brilliantly ingenious. It may even seem to be increased rather than diminished by seeing. This is partly because one is now much more aware of it and of its crafty operations, and partly because it is now cornered and making a desperate stand. Seeing does not change one's character overnight, turning a weak and erratic person into a resolute one: native temperament continues to make a lot of difference. Of course seeing does normally promote the dedication which is needed for its survival, let alone for its development. It demands complete dedication: there is no other way. It cannot be combined with any other purpose in life; it tolerates no other real interests. Compromise is impossible: one goes back, right back, at once. And then it is likely that one will suffer far more deeply than one who has never seen. There is no rest, no satisfaction, and not even the appearance of these, for one who has truly seen, except in the seeing. What matters is one-pointedness. Then there will be steady and perhaps rapid spiritual maturing.

8. Is this suitable for beginners?

Can this no-head experience be somehow induced in the spiritually immature, giving them the impression that it is all very easy? Can it not be a forced or copied thing, taken from another prematurely, without sufficient preparation? In that case, isn't it bound to be shallow and fleeting? These questions proceed from a misunderstanding as to what seeing is. So long as we are interested in getting experiences, instead of seeing this truth, this misunderstanding will persist. Seeing isn't getting anything whatever, but only getting rid of an absurd and damaging illusion; and this riddance can only do good, whatever the stage of our spiritual development. Just as you don't examine a specimen in the laboratory to get a scientific experience or for kicks, but to discover what it has to teach you, so you don't examine yourself in order to enjoy a mystical experience, but to see what you are, even if the sight should be very unenjoyable. Every human has the right of access to the truth about himself, whether he makes use of it or not.

Besides, who am I to say who is ready, and who isn't, to profit by the truth? Learned and pious old men can be spiritual non-starters, and boys can be almost Home. Of course, it would be unwise and futile (in fact, mere egotism) to press this truth upon people who aren't interested. But to withhold it for a moment from anyone who asks for it would simply mean that one had not seen it oneself. As for the results, they are not my business. The truth can be trusted to look after itself, in its own marvellous way and time. In any case, no-one will ever see it who isn't perfectly ripe and ready to do so: it just cannot be got over by any kind of persuasion. It is, in fact, quite incommunicable. Either you see it for yourself and by yourself, or not at all.

9. Is the no-head experience peculiar to one, or at most a very few?

To what extent is it valid, in just this form, for others? Five years ago, I should have said that, though the seeing itself is, of course, universally valid, this particular formulation could perhaps be of little help to anyone else: therefore it should be put forward with caution, and alternative formulations should be sought. The reason why I now take a different view is that there has been far more head-losing than I expected, with the results that I have outlined.

10. Is it Zen?

I have rather belatedly come to realise that it is not Zen. In its method (or lack of it), language, and style or flavour, it is no more Zen than it is Sufism or Taoism or mystical Christianity. It is thoroughly Western and 20th century, and presumably that is why it works here.

11. What is the connection between seeing and mystical experience?

Only when there has been much build-up of tension, or where the personality is of a certain type, is the initial seeing likely to be accompanied by some extraordinary 'mystical experience', with perhaps marked physical symptoms like trembling and sweating and weeping. Such an experience (it may take the form of an explosion of ordinary consciousness into Cosmic Consciousness, in a blaze of glory, love, peace, and joy) has no necessary connection with seeing. It may occur strongly and many times, long before one actually sees.

These brief occasions of Grace are unpredictable and beyond one's control, coming and going as they please. What comes will go. The essential seeing, on the other hand, neither comes nor goes. It is universal and indestructible, enjoyed unconsciously by everyone all the while. It is always accessible, because it is seeing what is always here and always clearly visible—one's Absence.

Having once seen This, one is never the same again, whereas even the loveliest and most devastating mystical experiences are apt to leave one very much the same. Or worse! When they are remembered and treasured, and their repetition is craved and worked for, they block seeing. In fact, they are capable of inflating the ego as nothing else can: they can become enormously head-swelling instead of head-shrinking or head-abolishing. Seeing provides nothing for the ego to feed on. It is empty, deflating, thoroughly humbling, even (in a certain sense) depressing. That is why it is 'difficult'.

And because This-which-sees-Itself is clean of all content, it is final and total and perfect, whereas 'mystical experiences' can always be bettered, explained, doubted, viewed from this angle or that. The richer they are the more vulnerable. Only the absolute Poverty right here is beyond all doubting, and has nothing to do with the anxieties and questions and comparisons of the spiritual game. Its score is Nil.

11. BANKEI

The Zen Master Bankei (1622-1673) was a maverick, an *enfant terrible,* whose life story in turn astonishes, and puzzles, and touches the reader. It is true that his insistence on the Unborn, which was his commanding insight and passion and theme, echoes the well-known assertion of the Buddha that there has to be an Unborn, a not-become, a not-made, a not-compounded, for there to be any escape from what is born, become, made, and compounded. Nevertheless to insist on any specific theme (let alone the Unborn) is so uncharacteristic of Zen that the Zen label hardly sticks at all to Bankei. The same applies to the practice which stems from his teaching. In fact it deliberately runs counter to the long-established and well-tried methods of the regular Zen sects that claim to set their face against any sort of attachment or rigidity or obsession. However, in spite of this untypicality—or more likely because of it—Bankei has recently enjoyed something of a revival.

Probably he owes much of his originality and independence to the fact that he was brought up as a Confucian before becoming a Buddhist. One of the Confucian classics, which he had to learn by heart, opens with the mysterious pronouncement: *The Way of the Great Learning consists in illuminating the Bright Virtue.* None of his teachers could explain what the Bright Virtue was, so he decided to find out for himself, whatever the cost. So for years, with this aim steadily in view, he subjected himself to incredible austerities. These included solitary meditation in a lonely hut for days and nights on end without sleep or food, mounted on a carefully chosen *pointed* rock which, having broken the skin, naturally prevented it healing.

At length, when he was 25, almost dying of hunger and exhaustion, the light dawned. Suddenly he realised that all along he had possessed the answer to the question that so tormented him. It seems that he discovered at that moment the common identity of the Bright Virtue and his own intrinsic Nature—the Unborn, the Buddha-Mind that is universally accessible and arranges everything to perfection. Abandoning all his austerities and making a miraculously quick recovery, he devoted himself from then onwards to living consciously from the Unborn, and teaching a fast-growing number of followers— many of them lay-people—how to do likewise.

The doctrine itself is simple and straightforward. Everyone inherits from his or her parents the Unborn and Undying Buddha-mind which is full of wisdom and takes good care of all things. To this unconditioned and unchanging Source of all are temporarily attached our separate names and identities, which are mere labels and quite secondary and derivative. When we are decisively convinced of this truth we see people as they are but we will appear inscrutable to them. Resting without strain or unnatural effort in this sure conviction, "with this Unborn Buddha-mind we can manage all things, and never be put in a false position or be led astray."

How do we know that we are all the while living from the Unborn anyway, whether we are as yet awake to it or not? By noticing how marvellously illuminating like a perfect mirror, it is. For immediately, without doubt or deliberation, it distinguishes between the bark of a dog and the chirp of a sparrow and the cawing of a rook, between red and green and blue, and so on *ad infinitum*. All sights and sounds, with their endless and striking distinctions, are the dynamic function of the Unborn. Our task through life is to become aware of this basic and mysterious function.

According to Bankei, this realisation of the Unborn is readily available just as we are now, in the comfort of our own home, and without undergoing the severe discipline of zazen or sitting meditation, to say nothing of the extreme austerities Bankei inflicted on himself. All that, he admits—wise after the event—was a mistake, a waste of time. For the Unborn is already alive and well right where we are, and just waiting to be taken up. The truth is that everyone is fully enlightened—yes, even wicked people are—without knowing it.

How is it, then, that we imagine otherwise? The reason, extrinsic to our True Nature, is social conditioning. And the remedy is to break free from this superimposed artificiality and be ourselves, the way we really are, just natural.

Better late than never, Bankei is now the enemy of all contrivance, of all needless ingenuity, and certainly of self-torture in Zen practice as well as in ordinary life. Thus he condemns the cultivation by Zen followers of "a great ball of doubt", and their obsession with koans, or deliberately baffling puzzles which don't arise spontaneously from within but are imposed from without. (Indeed, we can surely agree that five minutes of genuine inquisitiveness about our true identity are more likely to illuminate that identity than days and months of sitting meditation aimed at working up a spirit of inquiry by means of obscure devices imported from alien cultures and remote epochs, and laid on oneself by others; agree, that is to say, that no amount of sitting meditation guarantees any interest in the nature of the meditator, or in the Unborn that so thrilled Bankei.) Anyhow he assures us that we just have to "abide in the Buddha-mind, and then it is zazen all the time."

D. T. Suzuki wrote illuminatingly and with evident appreciation about Bankei's teaching: "Bankei strenuously opposed the koan method and called it down as an artificial device. In this he was like the followers of the Soto school, but unlike them he did not advocate silent meditation, the practice of which must have appeared to him just as artificial as the koan method... He told his followers to live by the Unborn with which we are all endowed as we come into this world. The Unborn is our own being as we have it prior to the world itself. In other words it is God before he came to be cognisant of himself."

Bankei's opposition to traditional Zen is more readily accounted for when we learn that, for some two hundred years, Japanese Zen had been declining. He could find no enlightened masters as guides, and so felt it was up to him to find the truth for himself. The outcome of his self-illumination was a type of Zen (or pseudo-Zen) that had a wide appeal. He quickly acquired a large following of ordinary lay men and women, as well as monks and nuns, and imperial recognition came in due course. His school flourished but did not long survive him. For obvious reasons Bankei Zen was attacked or ignored by the Soto and Rinzai schools. Thus he turned out to be the odd protestant whose reforms didn't stick, but were soon followed by counter-reformation.

Like most reformers, Bankei sought to simplify, to strip off centuries-old accumulations of artifice. But, unlike them, he didn't go back to beginnings, to the initial insights and methods of the founding fathers. It wasn't that he rejected Koan Zen and Sitting-meditation Zen in favour of the Original-face Zen or Seeing Zen of Hui-neng and his immediate successors, but in favour of his own brand of what we might call Metaphysical Zen.

The truth is that the contrast between the teaching of the great 9th-century Chinese Zen (Chan) masters and Bankei's Zen could hardly be more striking. Again and again he urges his disciples to cultivate the *thought* of the Unborn, to *believe* in the Unborn, to come deeply and steadily to *realise* that this is their True Nature and inexhaustible Resource. In effect he advocates switching from one *concept* to another concept, substituting for the *idea* that one has been born a particular and separate human being the *idea* that truly one is the Unborn and Undying Reality. We need, according to Bankei, *to change our minds* about our true identity, whereas Hui-neng and his successors urge us to see that we have no minds to change. They want us to drop all beliefs and opinions and simply to see our Original Face, our Void Nature, our Emptiness. This Seeing into Nothingness, according to Shen-hui, is the true and eternal seeing, and it's free of all thinking. Among those early Zen masters, Huang-po is the most insistent that our whole trouble is, precisely, conceptual thought, and our cure is to stop it and look directly into ourselves. He assures us that whereas the deluded many go by what they conceive, the wise few go by what they perceive. How unlike the teaching of Bankei!

One consequence of his frankly conceptual or metaphysical method was its popularity. At least to some degree a sort of Zen became available, without any special training, to anyone who was willing to believe in and hand over to the Unborn. Many people's lives were much improved, or even transformed, without their having to go through the devastating experience known as Satori. Just hearing about the Unborn proved enough, in some cases, to cause people to patch up family feuds, to cease worrying needlessly, to be kinder and more honest, to be better folk all round. One woman delightedly reported that when she came to be convinced of the Unborn she lost her fear of thunder! Again, how different is this polishing of one's human nature from the original Zen aim of laying aside that nature in favour of one's essential Buddha Nature.

However, it would be wrong to conclude that, because Bankei's Zen wears a popular face which readily lends itself to moralistic (and indeed homespun) applications, that his own enlightenment and that of his close followers was shallow or partial. As he himself points out, Zen takes all sorts of forms, and there are endless ways home to Where and What we really are. Evidently Metaphysical Zen suits some temperaments. Our Nature isn't fussy about whether we happen to arrive at it by looking to see our Original Face (No Face), by patient wrestling with koans, by long hours of zazen, by resting in the Unborn, or by any other means. Indeed Bankei is no inflexible dogmatist. Quite cheerfully he contradicts himself at intervals, and is refreshingly inconsistent in his instructions to his disciples. For instance, he easily slips into the traditional Zen doctrine of No-mind when he urges them to abandon all their ideas and *be stupid*. It's as if he handed on a knack of allowing the thought of the Unborn to put an end to thinking!

As for ourselves, it is surely clear that to suppress our habitual conceptualising and do away with ideas is both impossible and absurd, and if we think we are succeeding we are dupes of one of the sillier concepts. Demonising concepts is as unnatural and uncalled for as demonising feelings or sensations or percepts. The Universe is served up with generous helpings of all these vitamins, so to speak, and one needs a *balanced* diet. What one has to guard against is misplacing the items on the menu, as if one were spreading marmalade on one's fried plaice, or mixing caviar with one's custard. One's No-mind belongs right here where one is (and is not) at Centre, while one's Mind (along with its notion of the Unborn, etc., etc.,) is an outflowing or emanation from this Centre into region after region, everything arriving at and flourishing in its proper station. And this central No-mind or No-thing is one's ultimate refuge. To hang onto any idea (the nobler and profounder the more seductive) just won't do. It's literally for letting go of. Only its ineffable Origin, its nameless, featureless, unchanging Source, will never let one down.

Bankei himself observes that our Self-Nature, which is "empty and illuminating, is beyond the realm of thought." "Because the Buddha Mind is unborn, it has no thoughts at all." So in the end it appears that he, too, is well aware that to cultivate the *idea* of the Unborn is to root up its reality. There is little doubt that he would heartily endorse that fine saying from the *Chandogya Upanishad:* "Man gets satisfaction from the Unlimited, from the limited never."

12. SMOKE GETS IN YOUR EYE

Here's an example of what I call Visiotherapy—

I have noticed over the years that headlessness is a cure for smoking. It doesn't work in all cases, but there's a very good chance that when your head goes your cigarette follows, and your Eye opens.

The reason is clear. You began smoking because your cigarette or cigar or pipe confirmed that you had a two-eyed face here for that darn thing to stick out of. And the reason you went on smoking was twofold: the nicotine was addictive, and your two-eyed face still needed re-establishing. It remained in constant danger of vanishing.

And if you now give up smoking, the reason is equally clear. It's because your Central Void is even more addictive and your Single-Eyed Facelessness needs practising till it becomes a permanent realisation.

13. OUR ONLY PEACE

Here at my very Centre and Root, what I'm looking out of at you, is the Light which, as Dante tells me,

"makes visible
the Creator Himself to that creature,
who only in beholding Him finds its peace."
(*Paradiso* xxx.100)

By great good fortune I happen to be that creature, and so do you who distinguish the one on the near side of your mirror from the one on the far side. Here, right here where I AM, is the true and original Face of *THE* I AM, of Almighty God, which Face, in His infinite and astounding mercy, is at the same time my true and original Face. (My secondary and acquired face is the one on the far side of my mirror and in my passport, and His secondary and acquired face is the one in art galleries and children's books, complete with long snow-white beard against a long snow-white nightshirt.) Right here He and I are indissolubly and eternally united, and to prove it we wear one and the same vast and absolutely clear-complexioned Face. So it's no wonder that the sight of this amazing Face should be my ultimate and only peace. And that to overlook and neglect this Face (substituting for it that distant and obscure and practically invisible and fast-perishing acquired face) should ensure miseries piled high upon miseries. And be incredibly silly, if not suicidal.

Let me put the matter rather differently. It comes to me quite naturally to say "I am this or that or the other" any number of times a day. But the awesome truth is that in fact His I AM is indivisible, so that what seemed my tiny I Am is none other than His great big I AM. In other words, in graciously giving Himself to you and me, he gives the whole of Himself. Point blank He refuses to give you and me bits and pieces of Himself. He comes to us whole, or not at all. And what more vivid and always-present demonstration of this superb gift could there be than wearing the very same Face? And what happier vision? That's why it's called the Beatific Vision. It alone is our peace.

It's not much good just *believing* what Dante tells you, or I tell you, about the Beatific Vision and the Indivisible I AM. Two things are necessary. You have to see that Face of all faces, and you have to go on seeing it. You must practise seeing and wearing your divine-human Face. You have to keep trying it out and trying it on. You have to build up a new habit, the happy habit of enjoying the Beatific Vision. This is easy because it's natural and naturally addictive, at least as addictive as unhappy and unnatural habits like drugging yourself with alcohol or heroin or smoking fags.

At this point you ask me how well and for how long you have to practise this Vision before you enjoy the promised "only peace".

Well, my answer to this very reasonable question is a two-level one which runs like this. The *ultimate* truth is that your divine-human Original Face is your eternal and timeless Face, and the Peace that comes with it is yours from the very start, from your very first fleeting sight of that Face. Rest assured that He won't give you all of His Face and withhold the Peace that goes with it. Psychologists will tell you that your deepest and most powerful feelings can be those you are least aware of. So it is apt to be in this case. You clearly see your true Face, and think you lack the Peace that comes with the Vision. You don't. Would you exchange your deep peace for superficial peace? His will is your peace, and His will is that you be Oned with Him and share the same Face.

So much for that highest and deepest level which is beyond time, but of course we humans live in time also, and the question remains: how long do we have to practise seeing our divine-human Face, and practising that vision assiduously, before we bring to the surface the profound peace it engenders?

Well, I just don't know. We humans differ so much. From my very limited observation, it would seem that for most of us the practising-and-waiting period is a matter of years rather than months, but for some fortunate and gifted souls the practising-and-waiting period is quite short. For all you know, you could be one of them. In any case you may be sure of the peace which is so deep and so powerful that it remains unmanifest. Also you may be sure that there's nothing amiss with your Vision. To enjoy that Happy Vision for the very first time is to do so exactly as the Buddha and Jesus did after a lifetime of practice. This is the one thing you can't do wrong. You do it perfectly or not at all. Its brevity does nothing to tarnish its perfection. Here practice doesn't make perfect, it makes habitual.

If it happened that you were able to play the violin or the piano to perfection, or were able always to win at golf or tennis, I'll bet that you would lose no opportunity of exercising your prowess. Well, by the same token, exercise your prowess as a Seer, and trust the One you see to bring to your surface His peace in the right measure and at the right time.

Without this trust the beatific Vision wouldn't be beatific. A frown would disfigure those beautiful Features.

14. THE SEWING MACHINE MAN

Seymore Boorstein is a San Francisco psychiatrist who tells me the following story about the Sewing Machine Man. It's a true story, and it runs like this—

Seymore needed to have a sewing machine repaired and he took it to a well-recommended shop in another part of the Bay Area. Some surprises awaited him there. Displayed in the shop window and on the walls of the shop itself were a large number of cards bearing remarkably cheerful and encouraging messages, addressed to the public in general and particularly to customers. "Life is very, very beautiful", "The miracle of a blue hyacinth bulb's flowering tells us that there is Divine Goodness at the Heart of Nature", "You are a unique and marvellous person", "Bless you, dear friend", and much more of the same sort.

As a psychiatrist, Dr Seymore was of course hugely intrigued by these joyful and generous-hearted messages, and would have liked to ask their author—the owner of the shop, whose name, it seemed, was George—about them and himself, but the shop was extremely busy, and Seymore had to leave to keep an appointment.

But when he came back again a week later to pick up the repaired machine, a smiling George was available. He was a little man of about fifty, with grey hair, a heavily lined face and a limp. An ordinary-looking sort of fellow, one would say, that one would pass in the street without noticing him particularly.

He was very ready to answer Seymore's questions. Their conversation, as Seymore recounted it to me, ran along these lines—

S: I'm fascinated by the messages on the cards displayed in your shop and its window. You must have had a specially happy childhood. Tell me about it.

G: No sir! I had an awful infancy and childhood. My father was a raging drunkard who beat my mother and me, and my mother ran away when I was six. I don't know where she lives, or whether she's still alive. My life from six to twelve was spent in a so-called Home run by a pervert who regularly assaulted me. In fact, I don't think I could have had a much worse start in life.

S: Good Lord! How on earth do you account for your exceptionally happy and helpful state of mind nowadays? Please tell me exactly what happened to you and when it happened.

G: With great pleasure, sir. From leaving that so-called Home at the age of twelve, till I was twenty-five, I drifted around doing some casual labour, but also doing a spot of shop-lifting occasionally, as well as living on the dole. Yes, that was my real style—living on the dole. But, as luck would have it, I did eventually take some free training that was offered me in the servicing and repair of sewing machines. Thank the Lord for that!

S: What I want to know is what precisely it was that brought on the extraordinary change in your personality.

G: I was coming to that. At the age of twenty-five I was called up by the army. I remember that first day as vividly as if it was happening now, in front of my very eyes. Most of us recruits went in long-haired and bewhiskered, and none too clean, and dressed in all sorts of disreputable clothes, and I think I was the most disreputable character of them all. Well, we were stripped and thoroughly washed and given close hair-crops and clean-shaved and dressed in identical white shirts, and lined up on a long bench in front of a long mirror. Can you think what happened then? Happened to me, I mean?

S: No. Tell me, George.

G: *I couldn't make out which of those guys was me!*

S: Go on.

G: Well, I found out which of them I was by twiddling my right forefinger and pointing it at the face I used to think I had here, mounted on this very visible torso of mine. For some reason, not a hundred-per-cent clear to me, this experience on the long bench in front of the long mirror changed my whole life utterly. Actually I don't bother nowadays with the precise reasons for the change, but just get on happily with living the change, so to speak.

S: (after a silence of some minutes): What a marvellous story! It will take some getting used to. My first reaction was to invite you to come to my house and tell that story to some of my friends and patients. But on reflection that's a bad idea. Your place and job are here, and to my mind should not be disturbed. At any rate for the time being I shall content myself with recommending to all my friends this very efficient sewing machine establishment.

G: Thanks a lot, sir.

15. COSMAP

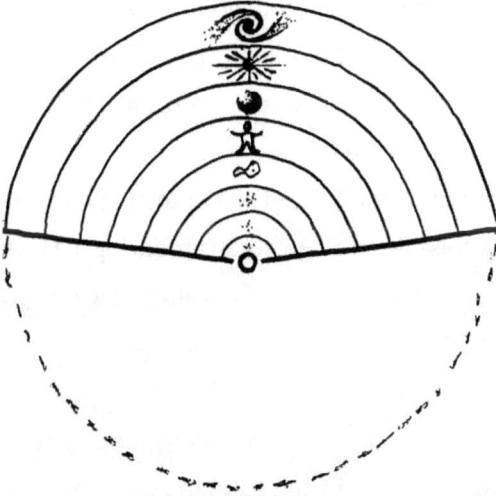

Without much justification, I used to think of it as my special brand of mandala. But on reflection this won't do. Unlike a mandala it isn't Buddhist, or Tantric, or Jungian, but something very different: it isn't a symbol but a map of the Self in the Universe and the Universe in the Self; it isn't symmetrical about a horizontal axis as well as a vertical axis but only about a vertical axis. On the other hand, like a mandala, it may be described as a visual aid to meditation that comprises a centre with its circumference, and between them a display of sacred or secular entities. But there the resemblance ends.

So I've decided, rather belatedly, to christen this offspring my Cosmap. And my purpose in this chapter is to take a fresh look at its history and its function, its validity and its effectiveness in the day-to-day practice and sharing of Inseeing, of the spiritual life generally.

In these contexts is it or isn't it (I shall be asking) something more than an optional extra?

First, then, its history and function.

By the mercy of God I eventually got off to a promising start. It was around 1940, when I had reached the age of thirty-one, that I decided it was high time I woke up to the identity of the character who had reached that advanced age in total ignorance of who had done so. With this end in view, I began producing the Cosmap in large numbers and great variety, all of them attempted self-portraits. And all of them based on the simple and obvious but basic proposition that what I'm taken to be is no fixture, but depends on *where I'm being taken in and looked at from, on the distance or range of my observer.*

For instance, observed from a distance of a few feet, I am a man all right. But move up to me, your eyesight sharpened with the right instruments, and I'm not a man at all but a huge and close-knit community of creatures called cells. Or instead move away from me, again armed with the right instruments, and I turn into one or another kind of geographical or astronomical being. And so on, up and down. Approach me and you come to what they say I'm made of, all the way down to whatever ultimate particles there may be. Retreat from me and you come to what they say I help to make up, all the way to whatever the ultimate Whole may be. But I say that in fact I'm all of these views of me, and that elastic!

And I have the findings of modern science, backed up by common sense, to confirm this impressive cosmic-cum-hierarchical portrait of myself and yourself. They encourage me to ask what this man is without his cellular population, and what each of his cells is without its molecular population, and so on down to what bottom there is to the system of wholes and their parts. And, changing direction, they encourage me to ask what remains of my precious humanness without the rest of Humanity? And go on to ask which do I need more—which is the more indispensable organ of mine—this right arm, or this planet with its air and water and soil and flora and fauna, or this sun with its energy and light? Which of these limbs or organs could I survive longer without? Which of them would be safer to amputate?

The inescapable answer to all such questions is that without the rest of the great hierarchy of wholes and parts a mere man is an abstraction and a nonsense. That to be a man he must also be the lot, from top to bottom and from bottom to top. That strictly speaking the cosmic hierarchy is indivisible. And that this Cosmap is a true portrait of myself.

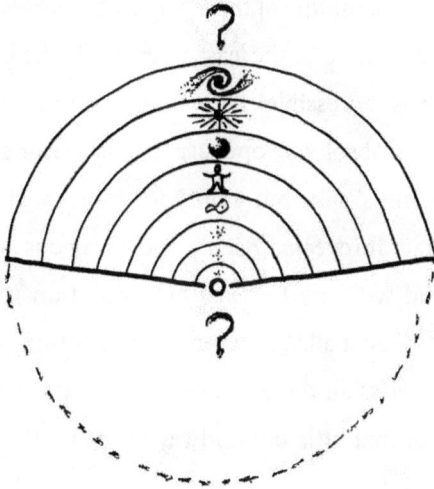

It isn't a map of a certain *terrain,* in the sense that an aerial photo is a map of a certain piece of country. It's the map of a *journey,* and a succession of terrains. It incorporates time, and is rather like a road-map that takes a long while to explore. In fact with its help and encouragement I'm playing the part of a cosmic traveller in search of himself. A traveller who, starting from some region beyond the galaxies, comes to regions successively solar, terrestrial, human, cellular, molecular, atomic, and subatomic. With some success en route (I may add) but none as yet at journey's end and beginning, as the question-marks indicate. It was as if I were pounding away at the door of my Peripheral Maximum and simultaneously at the little door of my central Minimum, seeking entry. And this pounding went on tirelessly but without effect for all of two years.

And then at long last the answer dawned, and both doors swung wide open. Suddenly it occurred to me that exactly where I found myself, the very spot I was looking out of, was by no means that human region in the middle of the Cosmap, but its very Centre. This Spot which I had taken to be the least accessible in the Universe turned out to be the most accessible! It lay *wide open* to my inspection— infinitely wide and absolutely open, specklessly clear and empty. Not empty for emptiness' sake but empty for filling with anything and everything. In fact It revealed Itself as No-thing busy exploding into Every-thing, and with joy I erased both question-marks from my Cosmap. I had made it all the way down to No-thing-whatever, and then (and only then) all the way up to All-things-whatever. That is to say: in spite of that little old midway human rather than because of him.

From that time on—for the past sixty years—the Cosmap, with minor variations from time to time, has served me well. It has, so to say, been my ground-plan, my working-drawing for use on the site. By no means a symbol or holy icon, but an ever-present reminder of my essential constitution. It connects me intimately with everything, it makes sense of my life, it gives me meaning.

Nevertheless I must now ask myself some awkward questions. Am I right to lean so heavily and for so long on what perhaps amounted to little more than an obsessive doodle? After all, the vast majority of liberated souls belonging to all the world's major religions managed very well with nothing of the kind. Could my precious Cosmap be my Costrap? It could well be seen as tethering me (albeit with a rather elastic rope) rather than freeing me.

Where can I go, to whom can I appeal, for reassurance on this vital matter? Somehow or other I must line up, if I can, my spiritual practice and discipline with that of the acknowledged masters of the spiritual life. I know of only one way of addressing this problem. It is to ask a very easily answered question: *How do I make these diagrams?* And of course the answer is: *With a pair of compasses.*

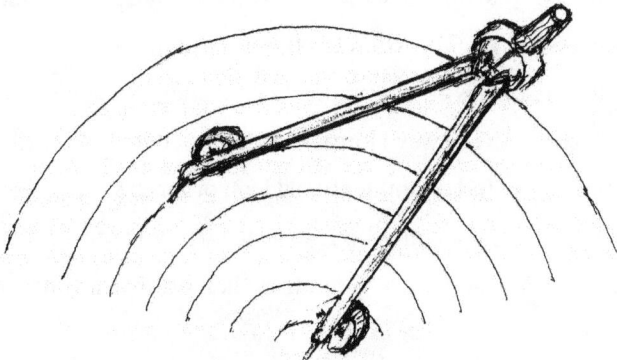

Yes indeed, I make my Cosmaps with a very common bipedal instrument, one foot of which is a fixed central pin while the other foot is a moving circumferential pen. THE ONE IS THE UNMOVED MOVER OF THE OTHER, NO MATTER HOW NEAR OR FAR IT MAY BE.

Which self-evident fact at once lines up the Cosmap with the great spiritual traditions, in the most concrete and practical fashion. In other words, without my realising it all those years, the Cosmap was in a peculiar sense the work of the Reality it sought to depict. Rather as if a portrait were stamped upon a canvas by the face of the sitter, or a book read itself out loud.

Let's say that if God is the Unmoved Mover of the world (and He is) then a humble pair of compasses is no less than *a very special bit of the divine anatomy engaged in the very special business of Self-portraiture.* He so kindly arranges it that I draw God, plus his Cosmos and Man (who is made in His image), by means of God. I draw God with God.

The result, no wonder, is that a whole bunch of puzzling questions are cleared up, as follows.

(1) My 60-year-old obsession with the Cosmap is revealed as a good obsession, an Obsession to end obsession.

(2) Its usefulness—its remarkable efficiency as a sort of spiritual *Guide Michelin* to the way Home—is accounted for. The truth is that it functions as a kind of unintentional icon or incentive to meditation, while remaining no symbol but instead firmly based on verifiable experience, on what's perceived rather than on what's conceived.

(3) The nest of concentric circles that looked so like a trap—and even a disease—turns out to be just the opposite. It's a vivid reminder and demonstration of the fact that I share with all those once-alien creatures a common Centre, so that I can and do say to every one of them: HERE I AM YOU! Now this, and this alone, I call true healing.

(4) Here's another crucial lesson the Cosmap's nest of concentric circles teaches me. Each additional circle that my compasses describe *encompasses and includes* the contents of the previous and smaller circles—with truly astronomical consequences. Our model of the cosmos is transformed. Thus the life and consciousness ON Earth becomes the life and consciousness OF Earth, and no longer a welcome guest or a not-so-welcome parasite. Equally the life and consciousness IN the Solar System becomes the life and consciousness OF the Solar System. And so on up to the Cosmos itself, which we have already described as One and strictly indivisible.

Nowadays, of course, everyone talks about our Living Mother Earth. But I have still to hear the astronomer's mathematical account of her journey round the Sun described as none other than her own account of it. And still to hear Mahler's *Song of the Earth* described as none other than her own musical soliloquy, her singsong.

Well, perhaps our Cosmap will one day help us to wake up to the shocking but inescapable truth that the life and consciousness in us is distributed throughout the cosmic hierarchy, and ultimately is none other than His—whatever name we choose to give Him or Her or It.

(5) Our Cosmap delivers from vagueness and wooliness—not to mention craziness—one of the most challenging and seemingly

absurd doctrines that recurs in the Upanishads and Zen and Sufism; namely that there is just One Seer in all beings, and that only God (alias our Buddha Nature or Source) really sees. From which it follows that people and animals as such don't really see each other. As Rumi says, to attribute sight to their eyes is like attributing sight to the eyes in a painting.

This is difficult to make sense of, still more difficult to incorporate in our daily life.

But again, God's compasses to the rescue!

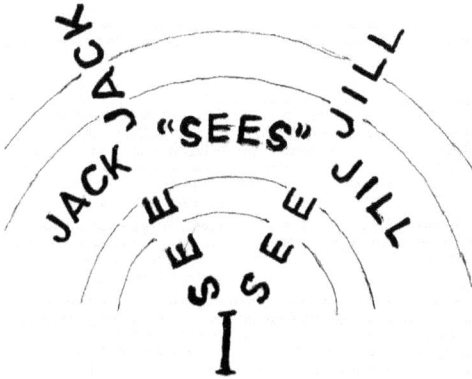

Whereas JACK "SEES" JILL is a circumferential and symmetrical and very human operation in which both parties stay intact, I SEE JACK, like I SEE JILL, is a radial and asymmetrical and divine operation in which I vanish without trace in his or her favour. When I rely (as I must) on present evidence, the two operations are radically different. And the question I have continually to put to myself is: which of them am I currently engaged in—the really real and divine sort or the far from real and very human sort? In other words, am I operating consciously from the fixed pin of God's compasses? Has what used to be a vague wondering and wandering become, thanks to the firmly-stuck pin of those compasses, a smoothly penned and steady path through life's problems?

Here, to put it mildly, is something more than a useful meditational aid.

(6) And that's far from all. Along with the transformation of my vision from circumferential to radial goes the abolition of my distance from all things whatever. Viewed from this pin-point all radii collapse to zero. Which is to say that, thanks to God's long-legged compasses, all things are encompassed, are mine, really are my very own. And to "underneath are the everlasting arms" I can now add "overhead are the everlasting legs". Not so beautiful, but very useful indeed!

With a view to being as precise as possible about the application of these discoveries to our every-day life, let us glance very briefly at the four stages of that life.

First, as new-born infants, says Wordsworth, "we come trailing clouds of glory from God who is our Home." And all the indications are that he got it right. As a radial Seer and not yet a circumferential "seer", the infant perceives no distance between himself and objects, and may be observed to clutch at and finger the Moon. Operating from the pin of God's compasses, he's the unmoved and boundless Space or Capacity in which things come and go, and in a true sense the Proprietor of them all. Of course they aren't yet elaborately organised, and he's unconscious of the Divinity he's living from.

Second, the young child, while still operating from the pin-point of his divine base, starts operating also from the moving pen-point of his humanness. Beginning to see himself as Jack who "sees" Jill, he has joined the Human Club. But this wonderful mix of God and man is all-too-brief.

The third stage of his life, as he approaches teenage and adulthood, is brought about by the coming adrift and slipping all over the place of his pin-point. The consequences are dire. His path through life goes all wobbly. The great world he so recently encompassed now encompasses him, and in it he's a stranger and afraid. The meaning of his life (which was his firm grounding and rooting in his divine Source) has vanished. Though he learns somehow to cope more or less bravely with a meaningless existence, the chance that he will stay stuck at this third stage—remaining a case of arrested development—are very great indeed.

The fourth and final stage is that of the seer and encompasser, of the central pin-pointer and peripheral pen-pusher who has taken up God's offer of union with Him at both extremities plus all that lies between—as roughly indicated on our Cosmap. Well, I can't speak for you, but I find the divine recourse to such a humble gadget as a pair of compasses, in order to accomplish his very special work with Mankind, as surprising as it's touching; also in strange contrast to all that subtle and complex and largely abstract theology.

Nor, incidentally, is this divine come-down unique. I'm thinking for instance of His Mirror and His Tunnel, devices whose important role in unveiling Himself figure prominently elsewhere in my work. He who fashions Himself—let alone innumerable universes all in working order—has this special toolkit that deserves our special attention.

Why?

Why because it's our special toolkit for returning the compliment and fashioning Him! He loves us doing that.

16. THE GLASSY ESSENCE SUTRA [1]

Man, proud man!

Dressed in a little brief authority –

Most ignorant of what he's most assured,

His glassy essence, like an angry ape,

Plays such fantastic tricks before high heaven

As make the angels weep.

Shakespeare, *Measure for Measure*

Hail to the Nirmanakaya, the Transformation Body which the Compassionate One assumes amongst humans to save them from disaster!

Thus have I heard:

The Blessed One was sitting alone and on high, timelessly absorbed in Incomparable Enlightenment.

Down below, aeons passed. At length a large company of Bodhisattvas, great and wise beings, came to visit Him. Aware of the rigours of their journey and the anxious concern that inspired it, He granted them immediate audience.

Their spokesman, the Venerable Ananda, began: "Lord, we are deeply troubled. The world of humans is going mad. Pride consumes them. Each craves authority and power over his neighbour, and each is given over to gross self-deception leading to suicidal strife and

---

1 Sutra is Sanskrit for sacred scripture. The Mahayana Buddhism of Tibet, China, Korea and Japan is open-ended. It recognises no fixed scriptural canon, and any proposed addition to its long list of sutras is to be judged on its intrinsic merits. Here I have followed more or less, their highly stylised form, in which the Blessed One, of course, is the Buddha that you really, really are.

woe. Not content with behaving like monkeys, they are behaving as monkeys might behave if they went crazy. And all because they lack the benediction of Your Holy Presence among them. The time has come, Lord, for You to bring Your infinite compassion to bear upon these deluded creatures. Descend, we beg You, from the heights, make Yourself available to all, and save them from themselves."

The Blessed One readily agreed. "For too long I have been remote and inaccessible. The time has come for Me to take on bodily form, so that, wherever these people are, there I shall be in their midst. Moreover they will have an infallible way of recognising Me. So different will this Body of Mine be from theirs that even the most purblind and unmindful of them could not help but pick Me out at once."

The Bodhisattvas were delighted, grateful, and very curious. Prostrating themselves before the World-honoured One, they said, "Tell us, Lord, what is the special shape You will take, what will be the distinguishing marks of the wonderful Transformation Body You will assume for the rescue of humanity?"

"I shall turn Myself into a Cyclops," He answered, "into a being with a single eye! All those folks peering and peeking at one another through a pair of tiny peep-holes apiece, and Me gazing steadily and clear-eyed out of one huge, speckless, frameless 'window'! That should make Me stand out so prominently it will be quite embarrassing."

The Blessed One made good His promise immediately. Taking on this striking and unique form, He turned up among humans everywhere and at all times.

And nobody noticed Him! People went on overlooking the Divine Oddity, the Cyclops in their midst!

The Bodhisattvas shocked and bewildered, could hardly believe it. "See how bemused and dreamy these folk are," they cried. "You will have to refashion Yourself even more drastically if You are to stand a chance of waking them up and attracting their attention."

The Blessed One was so astounded (not to say aggravated) by this news that in a flash He drew His great vajra sword and cut His own head clean off, single eye and all!

"As this abbreviated but still very much alive Being," He exclaimed, "how could I fail to stand out among all those unabbreviated ones? As this Unique Being who sees where there are no eyes and hears where there are no ears and tastes and talks where there is no tongue, I shall surely be the Wonder of the World!"

But No! Difficult as it is to believe, the only people who noticed— and dared to finger the perfectly-healed semicircular Wound He had inflicted on Himself—were some children who got laughed at, plus a sprinkling of adults. A sprinkling so small that it was lost like a five-minute rain-shower somewhere over the salt ocean.

His advisors were desperate. All they could do was to plead that He should re-model His Transformation Body still further, if possible in equally startling or more startling ways, so as to be sure of attracting attention anywhere and in any company.

Again he graciously agreed, and, after careful consideration, settled on the following additional measures.

"For a start, I shall turn Myself upside down. You notice how people have their heads on top, their bodies lower down, and their feet at the bottom of the picture. Well, I shall be the other way up! My feet shall go to the top, followed by My legs and My trunk, and finally My no-head down below. That ought to cause people to sit up and take notice.

"To make sure, I shall insist on V.I.P. treatment wherever I go. For example, when I stand on the seashore, the carpet of glittering light will unroll itself between the rising or setting sun and Me alone. Never will it lead up to anybody else. All vertical lines, such as the corners of the room I happen to be in, will visibly pay homage to My presence by converging on Me. My body will bulk much larger than the human bodies around Me, rather as the king in their old paintings is much larger than the servants and courtiers surrounding his majesty. And always I shall be at the very heart and centre of all things, and never let anybody push Me to one side.

In fact, I shall remain in the place where no change, no time, no death can enter, in the one and only timeless region. While everywhere else has its time-zone, its calendars and timepieces, none will be allowed in the place I occupy. Any watch or clock approaching Me and brought right up to Me, I shall magically cause to swell and grow dim, then illegible; and finally (when it has come all the way) non-existent. I promise that, wherever people meet, there among them will be the one spot which visibly stops all clocks. To find that spot will be to find Me, the Deathless One.

"So far so good, you may say, but what about something really spectacular? So be it. I will flaunt My divine powers to the limit, and mercilessly show up the feebleness of the creatures around Me. This

Decapitated One will forever be re-designing and destroying and re-creating the world in a flash and at will. How unlike those capitated creatures who—whether they look up or down or around, or rotate, or open and shut their peep-hole eyes—are powerless to change the scene one iota!

"But all this, of course, can be construed as unkind and ill-mannered and rude. To get rid of this idea, I shall come very close indeed to everyone, shall stand aloof from none. While all those creatures around Me keep their measurable distances from one another—each cold-shouldering the rest—I will stay distant from none. Even the longest tape-measure, stretched between them and Me, I shall visibly shrink to nothing, to a point, and so draw all to me, irresistibly, in the love affair of all time.

"Well," the Blessed One concluded, "what more can I do to win their attention and minds and hearts? Let's try this package deal on them, O Venerable Bodhisattvas."

They complied. The message was proclaimed everywhere. But of course nothing much happened. A few—a very few—took delivery of the package, and the plight of humanity grew worse. The Bodhisattvas were stunned, reduced to a kind of glazed and blinking trance.

All of them except Ananda, who was trembling so violently that the Compassionate One asked him: "Are you ill, Ananda?"

For a while Ananda seemed unable to speak. And then he blurted out in a rush: "Why don't they get it? I'll tell you why! Because what's noon-day obvious to all us Bodhisattvas is darkest night to them. O yes I'll tell you the reason! It's because they are blind to the most factual fact of all, the fact that TO GET IT IS TO BE IT AND TO SEE IT IS TO BECOME IT, and there's no other way. THE ONLY WAY TO SEE HIM IS TO BE HIM, AND THE ONLY WAY TO BE HIM IS TO SEE HIM. How I yearn to proclaim this news a million times in a million places!"

Having got this much off his chest, Ananda's trembling was a little reduced while he paused for a few moments to take breath. Then he went on as rapidly as before (addressing, it would seem, humans in general) "How could you ever find His single eye without looking out of it? How could you ever find His truncated Transformation body without taking on and being that same Body? How could you see all those other wonderful things He is and does without seeing that you are already being and doing and living from those very things yourself? Not, of course, because you deserve or have earned the tiniest bit of it, but simply because He has out of His infinite compassion bestowed them on you, made you that way."

"Calm down, Ananda," said the Blessed One, soothingly, "and when you are ready explain your meaning more clearly still."

Rather more quietly Ananda went on, still addressing the human race it would seem, "What are you most certain of? Not, surely, what you are looking at—which might be for all you know a waking dream, and in any case is a minute fraction of what's presumed to be there for the seeing. Not that! Not that! What can you be really sure of but what you are intrinsically, what's WHERE YOU ARE WHAT YOU ARE?"

Ananda stopped short again, still trembling somewhat. The others, having granted him a little rest, begged him to complete his message.

Which he did, as follows:

"Look now and SEE that What's central to you, What you are looking out of, your very Essence, is utterly transparent in all directions endlessly, perfectly clear, crystalline, glassy, unchanging, and moreover vividly aware of itself as This and quintessentially This. And all This is His, and This is Him, and This is What you are where you are What He is. And you and He are One for ever, for ever and ever. That which hitherto you were most ignorant of you are now most assured of—your Glassy Essence—and there's precious little danger of your behaving like an angry ape any more."

With that, Ananda's trembling was stilled, and his fever (if fever it was) ceased abruptly.

And in conclusion the Blessed One Himself graciously added:

"And if you—you who are now most assured of OUR Glassy Essence—fail to realise how your 'solitary' seeing into that Essence can and must somehow and sometime or other win over untold numbers of your fellow humans to this happy vision, let Me remind you that your seeing is none other than Mine. Place limits on That, if you dare!"

17. THE SEVENTEEN THESES

What is real is hidden from us,
But what is false is revealed as true.

Yoga Vasishtha

You shall know the truth,
And the truth shall make you free.

John 8. 32

We are all doing it right, living from our true nature, firmly rooted in reality, perfectly enlightened.

For sixty years I've been thinking about, writing about, sharing this stunning fact in all seriousness with anyone who will listen. And then, the sledgehammer! The extraordinary truth and joy of it hits me for the first time. Let me try to pass on to you something of my surprise and delight.

Strangely enough, this revelation dawned on me at what seemed a most unpropitious moment. I lay in hospital with a smashed hip and a twisted leg, and—as if that were not enough—a distended and aching stomach. Add to that, 93 years of wear and tear.

That was bad news, and I had a miserable time of it. On the subject of bad news, what news isn't bad? Switch on the telly, glance at the headlines. Could the current state of our species be more threatening? It looks as if man is truly bedevilled, and this man is by no means an exception.

In fact, I'll stake my eternal life and all I hold dear that we really are begodded, and our bedevilment is the most devilish of devilish fictions.

Prove it! I hear you saying.

Well, here are no fewer than thirteen proofs that we are really and truly begodded. No matter how foolish and weak and wicked we happen to be, I say—

(1) It is *impossible* for one not to vanish in favour of the person one is addressing, impossible not to give one's very life for the person. Confrontation is a thundering great lie.

(2) *Impossible* to box oneself up, to wall oneself in, to arrive at any limits whatever.

(3) *Impossible* to thing oneself, impossible not be be speckless, immaculate, absolutely empty for filling with whatever happens to be on display.

(4) *Impossible* to ward off anything, to refuse to take it on board, *impossible* not to explode, not to be all things because one is no thing.

(5) *Impossible* not to say and mean I, that first person singular present tense that is the One I.

(6) *Impossible* to drive one's car without (in fact) not driving the car at all but the countryside, the universe.

(7) *Impossible* not to be the One who takes on the pain of the world. Only here is it felt.

(8) *Impossible* not to live from the true centre of the universe.

(9) *Impossible* not to abolish distance, and coincide with the furthest star, the furthest galaxy.

(10) *Impossible* not to abolish time—where there is nothing to change there is no way of registering time, or time to register.

(11) *Impossible* to experience the beginning, interruption or cessation

of consciousness. All three are false. Time is in consciousness, consciousness isn't in time.

(12) *Impossible* not to look out of the boundless and undivided Eye of the One Seer, and that alone.

(13) *Impossible,* as a result of looking out of that Single Eye, not to exercise its power to destroy and recreate the world, at will.

And, as if this wealth of proofs of one's begodding or divinity were not immeasurably more than enough, here are four supplementary evidences.

(14) It is *impossible,* when standing on the seashore at sunset or sunrise, for the carpet of golden light not to be laid out for oneself alone.

(15) It is *impossible* to enter a room of which the vertical lines do not in fact converge on that infinity which is oneself.

(16) It is *impossible* to spread one's arms and not embrace the world.

(17) It is *impossible* not to transmogrify instantly any chair one sits in, turning it into the unique throne of the One, of God.

Seventeen proofs in all, whereas just one would have been enough to persuade any reasonable creature of his essential divinity!

What have the great sages and seers had to say about this crucial matter?

Take Eckhart for example. He got it right and he got it wrong. Again and again he says unconditionally that the true home of the living God is at one's very centre, from which one's humanity is absolutely excluded. God's in, Eckhart's out.

We are urged to put on our jumping shoes and jump into God, no matter who we are, how wretched and defective we happen to be as humans. Yes, but in other places he talks of the birth of God in the soul as an acquisition and dependant on our behaviour and merits. This birth "may take place in us and be consummated in the virtuous soul, whenever God the Father speaks His eternal word in the perfect soul. For what I say here is to be understood of the good and perfected man who has walked and is still walking in the ways of God, not of the natural undisciplined man, for he is entirely remote from, and totally ignorant of this birth."

Of course Meister Eckhart (in spite of such aberrations as this) was one of the world's greatest seers, and I never get tired of reading his incomparable sermons. Here, taken from them, are a few samples of his teaching at his unqualified best :

"God enters the soul with His all, not merely with a part."

"This birth happens just as much in a sinner as in a saint... Just pay attention."

"Since it is God's nature not to be like anyone, I have to become nothing in order to enter into His nature."

What I say is that we are all living from that central divine presence and doing so perfectly without fluctuation. Perfectly, perfectly! Perfectly, regardless of our awareness or ignorance of the fact, regardless of our behaviour. I defy anyone to deviate by a hair's breadth from our seventeen evidences.

My second example is the great Indian sage Ramana Maharshi. No doubt his teaching varied a lot, but on the central question of what I call our begodding he was as consistent as he was insistent. For example:

"What could be more concrete than the Self (the One)? It is within each one's experience every moment."

"There is nothing so simple as being the Self. It requires no effort, no aid. One has to leave off the wrong identity and be in one's eternal, natural, inherent state."

Disciple: "With all your penance for so many years what have you got?"

Ramana: "I have got what needs to be got. I see what needs to be seen."

Disciple: "Can all see the same?"

Ramana: "I see only just what all do. It is immanent in all."

"People do not understand the simple and bare truth, the truth of their everyday, ever-present and eternal experience."

I have a question here. Why is it that, of all the thousands of Ramana's disciples, no more than a handful have graduated from being disciples into being friends? And did so for the simple reason that they took him seriously, and realised that they saw no less and no more than he saw? Over the past forty years I have met, at his ashram in Southern India as well as in Europe and America, many hundreds of his disciples, but I have not so far met one who claimed to share his vision. In one way or another they all tell me that he alone arrived at that transcendent experience. Even during his lifetime he let them get away with this near-universal perversion of his essential message, and pretend the impossible.

Why did things go so wrong?

For three reasons. First, because he had paid a huge price in physical suffering for what turned out to be his own anyway, and people imagine, in spite of all his assurances to the contrary, that they would have to pay the same. Second, because of the heavy load of tradition that seems to make seership the rarest of attainments. And third, because he tolerated the lie that we are, as I put it, bedevilled. He didn't declare all-out war on what's so obviously false and bad, but contented himself with diplomatic protests, so to say. And the last of these reasons is the big one, which I want to develop here.

The Second World War provides an excellent analogy. Great Britain and France protested against Germany's rape of Czecho-Slovakia and Poland—to no effect. Their passive condemnation assumed a parity—even a moral parity—between sovereign states. Eventually they declared war—and the resulting cold war did nothing to challenge that parity and stop the rot. It was only when the hot war broke out that there dawned the vast moral disparity between the two sides and the beginning of the end. No longer verbal but actual and specific weapons were directed against actual and specific targets. Though a long while coming, victory was in the pipeline.

Great Britain and its allies compromised and compromised with the enemy, but came down hard and clean in the end. The sages and seers have still to do so. Eckhart had his brush with the Church, but did little to challenge its domination, and nothing to challenge the many deceptions embodied in language and other powerful institutions. As for Ramana Maharshi, it is difficult, if not impossible, to disentangle him from his venerable Hindu culture.

All the same, total war has been declared, and the enemy is in retreat, at least on a narrow front. Around twenty powerful weapons are being deployed against twenty different types of target—of social fictions—with complete success. And by weapons, I mean physical things that have to be moved around and deployed each in its own special fashion, just as if they were guns and tanks and planes and ships. Every one of them is specially designed to destroy a particular type of target. They are what we ususaly call our experiments or tests, and they include the tube, the card, the mirror, the spectacles, the in-pointing finger, the car that drives the world, the maps, and so forth.

These tests of our divinity or begodding, are normally used to structure our workshops (ranging from ten participants to upwards of two thousand at a time) as well as for showing any casual enquirer his or her true nature. Witnessing to their effectiveness are the following:

(a) Anyone who carries out the tests conscientiously sees clearly into his essential divinity. Just one test is enough to show him, strictly speaking, but more rub in the message, and people have their preferences. Of course what they do with their discovery is their affair. It may take a long while to win through, but in a more fundamental sense the war is already won, as I have shown.

(b) The tests are active, they do things instead of talking about them, and that is one of the reasons why they produce results, sometimes astonishing results.

(c) They are good psychology. Tell a man he's doing something very well—in this case perfectly—and he will persist in doing it. Tell him he's doing it very badly, and he will stop doing it.

(d) There really is an amazing amount of goodness around. Self-giving love and generosity keep breaking out. And no wonder, when you realise where they come from.

(e) Since everyone is really perfect at centre, there are no elite, no spiritual bosses. One has (or should have) equal respect for all humans.

(f) The discoveries that the tests reveal are entirely compatible with science.

(g) The heart of the universe is sound. The true news is good news, amazingly good news.

Jesus ticked off the man who called him Good Master. "Only God is good," he assured the man. Yet he tells us elsewhere to "be perfect even as Our Heavenly Father is perfect."

How to reconcile these two pronouncements?

This way: our 17 perfections (with others lurking, no doubt) are in fact God the Father's bestowed on us by grace, and it's time we started pouring out our hearts in gratitude to Him and living accordingly.

18. BALL GAMES

Robin Moulsdale is a good friend and a dedicated seer into his true Nature. The form his meditation takes is ball games in general and golf in particular. Yes, while his hobby is bird-watching, ball games structure his spiritual life, so to say. That's why, when he stayed with us recently for a couple of days, we were able to entertain him as royally as he deserves.

Let me explain. Our house borders on the wide mud flats of our Suffolk River Orwell, which are rich and noisy with the chatter of many species of waders, AND Robin's visit happened to coincide with the snooker masters' final between Hendry and Williams which Williams won. A double treat for Robin, whose home in Shropshire, though on the telly all right (or do I mean all wrong?), boasts no mud flats whatever.

For good measure, Robin and I had an exciting and indeed crucial topic of conversation. Perhaps I could sum up our conclusions like this: we wholeheartedly agreed that *spirituality* is a terribly tricky term and takes innumerable forms, most of which are as a rule (but quite wrongly) reckoned to be just about as secular and unspiritual as they come. One isn't in the habit of attributing to the top ten snooker masters a spirituality on a par with or superior to one's own. Williams is in no danger of canonisation. *Yet why not?* When he's on form and is, as they say, "in the zone", his long pots and his positioning for the next pot and his snookering are as miraculous—and certainly much more abundant—than the miracles which the Catholic Church sees as evidence of sainthood. I'm told that most snooker masters practise for hours every day. Now there's dedication for you! Furthermore, as saints have their devotees so snooker masters have their fans. Ronny O'Sullivan and Jimmy White, for instance, fill huge arenas with adoring spectators, intent on the niceties of every shot. I'm reminded of mediaeval times when the hunt for relics of the saints, and for sacred objects in general, amounted to a major industry, and the setting up of the hallowed remains of Christ's cross must have required the cutting down of forests. Things have changed a lot since those far-off days of course, but not all that much. I wonder how much a dedicated Ronny O'Sullivan fan would fork out for the very cue with which Ronny won his Benson and Hedges final, duly autographed and complete with cue-case and an icon of the master.

Now add to all of this crypto-spirituality the strong impression I get from watching these masters (yes, my wife and I are eager TV viewers of snooker) that their lifestyle has produced what we call strong characters, used to and ready for much defeat no less than for occasional victory. Add all this together and what have the saints got that the snooker masters haven't got?—except *consciousness of sainthood,* which consciousness certainly subtracts mightily from sainthood.

Admittedly the form which the snooker masters' pseudo-spiritual practice takes can be described as peculiar and arbitrary, but again no more peculiar and arbitrary than Robin Moulsdale's golf. And certainly no more so than Pure Land Buddhism, which has a large number of followers in Japan. Unquestioningly they believe that their simple faith in the Bodhisattva Amida and their prayers to him ensure easy and certain re-birth in the Western Paradise and Nirvana attained.

By way of contrast there is the Russian Pilgrim's prayer "Lord be merciful to me a sinner", repeated without ceasing day and night till the words come to repeat themselves automatically. Whether they then retain any meaning at all is a good question. Don't tell me that this practice is more spiritual than Ronny O'Sullivan's snooker practice.

In truth, what matters isn't the form which one's "spiritual" practice takes but the spirit in which it's undertaken.

The forms which the true spirituality takes vary widely and wildly, but the spirit is the same, the same, the same the whole world over. Let us stay awake to this fact and we will find that our precious notion of what spirituality is has burst its bonds, and become world-wide and million-faceted. It would make no real difference to our meditation if it consisted of repetitive gobbledegook, so long as it was pursued with sufficient dedication.

As for the actual form our own spiritual practice is going to take, there's no telling. I believe that every creature who says "I AM this and that and the other" (which, as Meister Eckhart points out, only God can truly say) is a unique and indispensable component of God's Universe. You may have to wait quite a time to find out what your unique contribution to the Whole really is. It took me thirty-three years before I discovered for certain what I had come into the world to do. And I find it impossible to exaggerate the difference that discovery has made to my life: in fact, it has bestowed meaning on what had been a meaningless existence. Was it Plato who said that a life without meaning isn't worth living ?

But just a moment! To be fair to saints and sages, the real ones do have something precious that snooker masters (as such) lack. And that is consciousness of their Source and of their union with that Source, together with a vivid consciousness of the "impossible" miracle of the Source's own Self-origination. You could say that the snooker master's ignorance of his sainthood is a plus that does much to cancel out the minus of his ignorance of his Source and Origin. Ideally, I suppose, one would be like Robin Moulsdale, who happily combines his ball-game with his "spiritual" game.

Ball games are by a long chalk the most popular and varied kind of game. The varieties I can think of are—

Baseball, Bowls, Cricket, Croquet, Fives, Golf, Hockey, Lacrosse, Marbles, Ninepins, Netball, Rugby, Snooker, Soccer, Squash, Tennis of the Court kind and of the Table kind, and Volleyball. And doubtless there are others.

Now I ask myself what's so special about ball games that accounts for their outstanding popularity and variety?

So far, I've come across the following answers—

The price of entry to the Kingdom of Heaven is to become like a little child. In fact, to revert to one's own childhood. What better way of doing so than to play ball?

In his myth of the origin of the sexes, Plato pictures a man and a woman as originally united in a kind of ball, happily rolling along.

Then they were split along a jagged line and set face to face, so that each became, so to say, only half human. Now the severed parts spend their time looking for "their better half" and occasionally finding him or her. Now men and women are, as Shakespeare says in Sonnet 94, "lords and owners of their faces". You have read (or are about to read) much more on the subject of faces, and face-to-face confrontation, in other chapters of this book.

A ball is a uniquely *simple* object consisting of one thing or element, not complex or divided, plain, unpretentious. As such it is a uniquely fitting symbol and manifestation of the One that is Simplicity itself. I think it was St. John of the Cross who said that only God can be perfectly seen because only God is perfectly simple. Certainly it was Carl Jung who pointed out that simple things are the most difficult. And of course there's that well-known passage in T. S. Eliot's *Four Quartets* about our inability to bear much simplicity.

In my end is my beginning, the wheel turns full circle, and, as Edgar tells Gloucester in *King Lear,* "ripeness is all". What more appropriate symbol and expression of this maturing is there than the revolving ball?

"Nothing brings me all things" says Timon in Shakespeare's *Timon of Athens.* Exactly so! A well-turned and well-balanced match-quality snooker ball is a beautiful miniaturising of this profound statement. In fact, such a ball comprises first a one-dimensional O or zero, then an infinite number of two-dimensional circles, each standing at an infinitely small angle to its neighbour on either side; and the joint result is three-dimensionality. Now there's magic for you!

Like my English friend Robin Moulsdale, my American friend Michael Murphy finds his spirituality taking the form of golf (Michael and I worked together at Esalen and in San Francisco in the Make-love-not-war era.) In his book *Golf in the Kingdom* (Latimer, New Directions) he writes—"Golf is played at many levels. Take our love of the ball's flight, the thrill of seeing it hang in the sky. How many games depend upon that thrill—archery, football, golf—the thrill of a ball flying to a target, have you felt it? The ball flying *into* the target: it's a symbol, of course. The flight of the ball, the sight of it hanging in space, anticipates our desire for transcendence. We love to see it hang there, that is why we love to hit our drives so far. The ball in flight brings dim memories of our ancestral past and premonitions of the next manifesting plane. The thrill of seeing a ball fly over the countryside—especially over a stretch of water—and then onto the green and into the hole, has a mystic quality. Something in us loves that flight. What is it but the flight of the alone to the alone?" (I have condensed Michael's text just a little.)

Brian Groves, an English friend of mine, has spent much time coaching young cricketers. He writes: "I must say that after reading *Head Off Stress* (one of Harding's books) and carrying out the exercises therein, my batting has improved no end. When asked to fill the bill when my young cricketers were a man short, on two occasions I have scored hundreds, which in my salad days (I am now 68) was an event that seldom occurred."

A headless friend of mine, Lew Monte, was till recently one of the top tennis coaches in America.

I guess that, like me, you have marvelled at photographs of the Milky Way which resemble a vast dusting of the finest flour, in which every flour-grain is a star. These photos give us some idea of the billions of stars that comprise God's fabulous Universe. Also some idea of the billions of those stars that doubtless have developed into solar systems that support living forms fantastically different from the human form—eyes and antennae and arms and legs sprouting from all over the body. Countless numbers of these weird creatures, lots of them far ahead of us intellectually and spiritually, no doubt, but saying with us the equivalent of "I AM this and that and the other". Now the marvellous thing is that you and I who see into our Divine Nature see also into their Divine Nature, and we are One with every one of them in the One, all physical differences notwithstanding!

This fabulous Universe is God's very own Ball Game. And when I say *Game* I mean an operation so serious and so severe that He fell in love with us His creatures, and the cost to Him of that Love was immeasurable. And now all our little ball games are subsidiary to, and derive from, His own archetypal Ball Game of Love. Their purpose is to direct us to Him Who lives and loves in our very heart, as the Whole of His strictly indivisible Being.

All that I aim to say in this chapter is very beautifully expressed in Meynell's poem *Christ in the Universe,* which concludes with these lines—

But in the eternities
Doubtless we shall compare together, hear
A million alien Gospels, in what guise

He trod the Pleides, the Lyre, the Bear.
O be prepared, my soul!
To read the inconceivable, to scan
The myriad forms of God those stars unroll
When in our turn we show to them a Man.

We are made in the image of God. It follows as the night the day that He's made in our image, and we are, as St. Peter reminds us, partakers in the Divine Nature. Not only does God watch snooker finals as eagerly as we do, but His Universe is very aptly described as His snooker game—how often has He cruelly snookered you?—Yes but, realizing that at Root and Centre you are Him in His Entirety, you are at the end of the day a snooker master, a finalist, and a certain Winner.

19. ERNST MACH AND CO, LIMITED

Primarily this chapter is about the German Professor Mach and what he called his Diagram. Nevertheless, so far as I'm concerned, the story begins with an English professor in an English university, and ends with another English professor in the same university.

The reason for this shift of scene is that I was a student at the same English university from 1927 to 1931, and it was through my contact there with Professor Karl Pearson and his work that (in the fullness of time) I chanced on Ernst Mach, whom Pearson admired as much as I do. Pearson wrote a book in the Everyman series entitled *The Grammar of Science* in which he reproduces Mach's Diagram, and I'm as eternally grateful to Pearson for doing that as I am to Mach for making the Diagram in the first place.

Why?

Because that so-called Diagram changed my life.

Here's a copy of it—

When I was a student at University College, London, Karl Pearson was the Galton Professor of National Eugenics there. (Before that appointment he had been Professor of Applied Mathematics and Mechanics in the same college.) I well remember visiting his department and coming across an account of a family whose name was (I think) Jukes. They were all physically and mentally defective, and very prolific. This upset Pearson the eugenist, who thought something should be done about it. This was before Hitler's "racial cleansing", which has of course (and so rightly) given eugenics a very bad name indeed.

All the same, I owe to Pearson, I repeat, my introduction to Mach, the man who made a huge difference in my life, confirming and completing with his Diagram the insight that had been my overruling passion from childhood.

It happened this way. For all sorts of reasons, I had become convinced that the key to my problems and my healing was to turn my attention round and *look at* and take seriously what I was *looking out of*. Convinced that at the very Centre and Home Base of each of us lies his or her cure, and the cure of the terrible anguish of our world. Yes, that was my deep conviction, long before I chanced on Mach's Diagram.

Yes, but to be convinced of something isn't at all the same as seeing it. Mach's Diagram introduced me to what's actually on show at my Centre, to the headless human body I'm actually looking out of. I once was blind, but now, thanks to Mach and his admirer Pearson, I see.

In point of fact, it wasn't while I was at UCL that I discovered Pearson's *Grammar of Science* with the Diagram in it, but much later. When, because of my old connection with its author, I bought the book, I was all of 33, and serving as a wartime officer in the army in India. I'm writing this chapter at the age of 94, and the sixty-one years between then and now have (apart from some deplorable but brief lapses) been devoted to practising and sharing my rather different version of the Diagram with people all over the world. By some miracle I managed also to earn my living as an incidental sideline—and quite a decent living, at that. My instinct is to attribute this miracle to divine Grace, which is a very unMachian thing to do.

For Ernst Mach was a dedicated opponent of metaphysics and deductive philosophy, and of course all religious dogmas. For him they were meaningless twaddle, and the only brand of philosophy that made sense was inductive. Which insisted on verifying by means of sense experience all the propositions of science. But more of that later.

Meanwhile a few words about the man.

Ernst Mach was born in 1838 in what is now Czechoslovakia, and died in 1916 in what is now West Germany. And he grew up to become in turn an eminent mathematician, physicist, philosopher, and experimental psychologist. In 1864 he was appointed professor of mathematics in Graz University, Austria; then from 1867 to 1895 he was professor of physics at Prague University; and then from 1895 to 1901 he was professor of inductive psychology at Vienna University. So much for his academic career. Posthumously, in the 1920's, his work contributed largely to that of the Vienna Circle, an influential group of thinkers who laid the foundations of logical positivism, which came to enjoy a great vogue in English and American universities. And of course he's generally familiar as giving his name to the Mach Number, which is the ratio of the speed of an aircraft to the local speed of sound.

Moreover, to cap it all, it's said that he was a brilliant and popular lecturer because of the force and clarity with which he presented his ideas.

In short, he's what they call a polymath. That's to say: a person who excels in a whole range of sciences and arts.

And he happens to be someone I couldn't agree with more, and couldn't agree with less!

First let me explain what Mach and I agree about:

His case as I see it (and mine) is that if there's no way to test a proposition it's not worth testing: it amounts to meaningless nonsense at worst, or a species of poetry or pleasant noises at best. Verify it if it's true, demonstrate its falsity if it's false. And just how do you do these things? Mainly by looking at it, but also by touching it, smelling it, tasting it if possible, listening to any sounds it's making. In other words, by noticing and attending with special care to exactly what it is that's presented to your senses, attending to the primary, unedited data, to what's actually given, before it's moulded and all distorted into socially acceptable shape. Before it's conventionalized —sometimes out of all recognition.

Let's take an example of how Mach proceeds in his own kind of rigorous empiricism. Having closed his right eye, he makes his Diagram of what's presented to his left eye, and he describes what he sees as follows:-

"In a frame formed by the ridge of my eyebrow, by my nose, and my moustache, appears a part of my body, so far as it is visible, and also the things and space about it." *Analysis of the Sensations— Antimetaphysical, The Monist, vol. 1, p. 59.*

As I have already said, I owe a huge debt to Mach for his Diagram, but I have to say that it was not nearly radical enough. He broke his own rules, cheated, cooked the books. Closing his right eye amounted to gross interference with the primary data. The natural and completely honest thing to do is to close neither eye but to look out at the world as we all normally do, through both eyes simultaneously, and make the crucial discovery that for the first person they merge into One Boundless Eye.

The result of Professor Mach's failure to live up to his own principles was, I find, startling. He produced one artificially opaque nose on the right side of the "face" he no longer had. Just one very large and very solid proboscis. Whereas, if he had kept both eyes open, he would have discovered that he had two noses, one on either side of his "face", and both of them beautifully transparent.

I warmly invite you, my reader, right now, to look, without turning your head, as far as you can to your right, and then as far as you can to your left, and verify the fact that (now you are no longer mucking up what's given) you truly are the proud possessor of a pair of huge and perfectly transparent noses, one on each side of your "face". Notice the miscellaneous objects that each of those noses contains. As for myself at this moment, my left nose contains a television set and a tape recorder, and my right nose a gramophone, a bit of a grey wall, and a picture.

What do yours contain?

In fact, there's more than a whiff of artifice, of cheating and cooking the books, about this strenuous peeking to the right and the left. The natural and uncontrived thing to do is what we all normally do do, which is to look more or less straight ahead. And then, of course, you are noseless and headless. As you can see you are at this moment, provided you take the trouble to look in at what you are looking out of.

Just why is this rather pernickety twin-nose discovery so important? you may well ask, indignantly.

Because, I reply, of its immense practical consequences. Over the past sixty odd years I have met and made many friends world-wide who, enjoying and practising this and similar discoveries in radical empiricism, live radically changed lives. They have come to discover their identity at Root with what I call their Divine Origin.

How was it that Mach and Co. fell so far short of their own radical principles.

I don't know enough about Mach himself to say, so I think the best way to answer this important question is to turn now to the most eminent exponent of logical positivism in England—A.J. Ayer (1910-1989)—who in 1946 was appointed Professor of the Philosophy of

Mind and Logic at University College, London, some years after I had left that seat of learning. I never met him, though we did have some brief correspondence.

Professor Ayer hasn't a clue to what he's missing by failing to put his own principles to the test.

One last example of the twenty or so tests or experiments that we have devised so far, and their application to our Professor—

Sitting at his desk in his office in UCL, Professor A. J. Ayer finds himself ensconced within stately and well-built walls which are certainly vertical. Now if he were to take a metre rod and use it to prolong downwards the corners of the room, he would find that, instead of meeting (as Euclid says) at Infinity, they met in himself! Which is as much as to say that, as first person singular, present tense, he's none other than the Infinite Itself! Also he would find that every room in UCL, every room in his own house, in fact every room he happens to enter, is collapsing, There's a profound lesson lurking in this discovery.

The long and the short of the matter is that, when you muck about with what you see, with what's actually given, you make a Diagram of yourself. That's what you reduce yourself to. Whereas, when you submit to what you see in all its unspoiled native vigour and blessing, you make a Portrait of yourself. Of Your Truly True and magnificent Self.

Which is what we regularly do in workshops. Here, for example, is a copy of a Self portrait of an 8-year-old girl, vis-à-vis a friend.

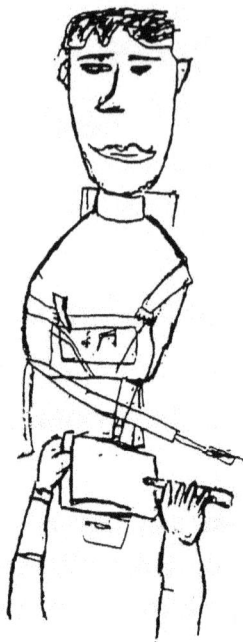

Notice the huge *physical* difference between the first-person artist and her second-person model. And how the former is operating from unlimited space, while the latter is just one of the objects inhabiting that space. No doubt the artist will grow up (as nearly all of us do) to trade her space for her face—what a deplorable deal!—but let's hope that its dire consequences will eventually drive her to revive her child's wisdom.

Here's a poem by another little girl I knew called Karen, who was nine at the time:

Have you ever felt like nobody,
Just a tiny speck of air,

With all those people around you.
And you just aren't there?

Now here, by way of conclusion, is a nosegay of blossoms plucked at many times in many places—

The foolish go by what they think rather than by what they see. The wise go by what they see rather than by what they think. Huang-po
He who doubts from what he sees will ne'er believe, do what you please.
William Blake

The aspects of things that are most important for us are hidden because of their simplicity and familiarity. Ludwig Wittgenstein

The Purloined Letter, in Edgar Allan Poe's story of that name, *"escaped observation by being excessively obvious. The villain deposited the letter beneath the nose of the whole world, thus preventing any portion of the world perceiving it."*

The Sage all the time sees and hears no more than an infant sees and hears. Lao-tzu

Anything, however small, adhering to the soul, prevents your seeing me. Meister Eckhart

Sit down before the facts like a little child, and be prepared to give up every preconceived notion. Follow humbly wherever and to whatever abyss Nature leads, or you shall learn nothing. T. H. Huxley

20. THE COMPASS

Mankind has lost its way.

And no wonder. The compasses it's using point only North and not also South, and therefore aren't compasses at all. They point at random, in any direction. Compasses that work are diamond shaped and just as good at pointing South as pointing North. Which, being interpreted means: they point simultaneously at the perceived Object over there and the perceiving Subject right here at one's Centre.

Even when a pseudo-compass or half-compass happens to be pointing to the Subject it turns that Subject into an Object. For instance, when I'm confronted with a human being I'm terribly apt to say that I'm face-to-face with that human being, in a symmetrical Object-to-Object relationship. So far as I can discover, in all the languages on Earth this reaction is expected of me. Very, very few people are observant and daring enough to say NO! The true (and indeed blazingly obvious) relationship is that person's face over there *vis-à-vis* the conscious Space or Emptiness right here—this Emptiness for filling with that face, as well as anything else that happens to be on offer.

In fact, it's quite impossible for me (or anyone else) as First Person Singular to confront anyone. Truly speaking, I have never faced anyone in the whole of my long life. We are all built to vanish in favour of the other fellow. A wonderfully courteous and generous thing to do! Just think of the transformation of our sick society that would happen if only half of mankind started using a true and diamond-shaped Object-Subject compass!

At this point I seem to hear you raising some objections, which I'll now do my best to answer.

The first is this. I who raise objections can and very often do look down at my body. I can draw it or photo it, for the simple reason that it's an Object which is every bit as objective for me as *your* body is for me. You and I match up quite nicely.

To which I reply with a question: WHERE ARE YOU? Or let me put it this way. What part of this body of yours is missing here, are you unable to objectify? I suggest that it's right here in and as that missing part that you are stationed, in the Place which is your Base and Home Ground and of course yourself as Subject. Something like this—

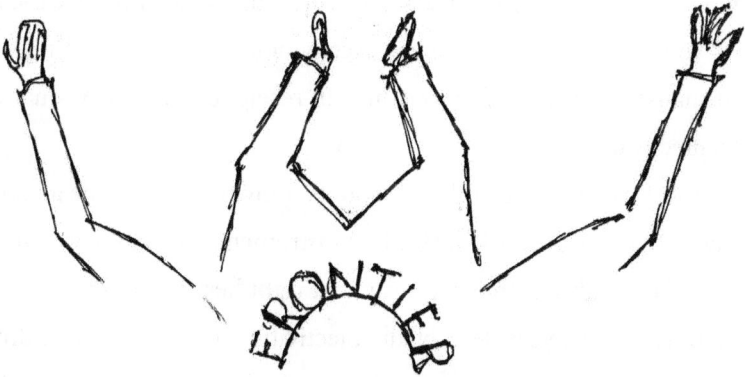

To your further objection that there's something marginal or inadequate about this Subjectivity, I suggest that you take a good look at it—at this Emptiness-for-filling right where you are stationed. And then I feel pretty sure you will find that it's wide awake, boundless, infinitely capacious, undying, the Unmoved Mover of the World. And may I add that you would be hard to satisfy if That didn't suit you?

In case you ask me to point out the exact Boundary where the objectifiable part of your body ends and your Subjectivity takes over in all its magnificence and benediction, as very roughly indicated in my sketch, I would draw attention to the semi-circular, left-to-right frontier where the index finger-nail of your touching hand disappears.

And in case you should still tell me that appearances are deceptive, and you and I *really are* face-to-face, I say to you: In the eyes of all the world that is true, because for them we are 3rd Persons, whereas for us one or other of us is First Person Singular, and the First Person is by definition and experience Subject. And if you don't believe me I ask you just how you could be in receipt of my face in its well-nigh-inexhaustible detail if you were also in receipt of your own equally detailed features?

And further, if you still have doubts, I invite you to come all the way up to me, armed with all the best instruments, and check whether I'm speaking the truth when I say that right here what I'm looking out of is pure Subject clean of all objectivity. If you will then kindly, on arrival here, turn around and instead of looking in at me look out with me, I am confident we shall share a Common Subjectivity.

If you feel you need moral support for this adventure, you can find it in plenty among the great sages and seers of the major religions, who insist that this No-thing-Everything at everyone's inmost Centre is none other than their Source, the Power and the Glory from which all things arise.

To which let me add that THIS, and THIS alone, can (I have come to believe) be trusted in the longest run not to give you and me what we want but what we need. I'm not asking you to believe this. But it might be a good idea to try it out.

21. THE DARK TOWER

"Childe Rowland to the Dark Tower came" is surely one of the most magical lines in all English literature. Robert Browning took it for the title of a poem in which he goes on at length and in detail about the miseries and dangers of the wilderness he finds himself wandering in—a wilderness dominated by a great Tower. Some believe this Tower is the lair of an Ogre who entices wayfarers, only to gobble them up instantly. In fact, Browning lifted the line from Shakespeare's King Lear, where it's spoken or sung by Edgar who's feigning madness. "Fie, foh, and fum", he adds, "I smell the blood of a British man."

Browning borrowed his title from Shakespeare, and I borrow mine from both of them. With a nod in the direction of Lord Byron also, who wrote a number of cantos about a young Dark-Age prince called Childe Harold, which included a large element of autobiography. In this chapter I follow a similar pattern.

I find myself homeless and lost in a flat and monotonous country, much of it wasteland. It's a backward country and very poor—often famine-stricken—and always dangerous. Hate and violence rule here. But perhaps the most depressing feature of this featureless land is its hopelessness, its lack of purpose and meaning. At least in this sense it lies in the middle of a Dark Age.

But no Dark Age is pitch-dark. There's just one thing that stands out and offers some glimmer of hope in this otherwise hopeless land. And, yes, it is the Dark Tower. To the Dark Age its Dark Tower. True, its windows are few and iron-barred and small and very high up, but they do from time to time send a brief but brilliant light far into the prevailing gloom.

What goes on inside this peculiar and occasional lighthouse?

No-one knows for sure. But of course there are many and conflicting rumours. It's variously reputed to be a strong Fortress against all danger, a Temple of divine wisdom and beauty, a Hospital or *Hotel Dieu* for healing spirit and mind and body, and the Palace of the de-throned King of the whole land. So some say, hoping against hope. But they go on whispering stories about the appetite of the Ogre.

At least the Dark Tower holds out the possibility that it conceals a unique cornucopia of good things. But in that case why do quite sensible people pretend it's a mirage, if not totally non-existent? Why on earth, if it could house the Light that would light up our Dark Age, is it for the most part ignored, rubbished, avoided like a man-trap or pest-house? Is this rejection mere folly (if not downright madness) on our part, or is there perhaps a very real Peril lurking in the forbidding structure, a Menace that's even more forbidding? Is there an Ogre, after all? Some, scared out of their wits, claim they have seen and been chased by him.

Perhaps there is a basis for the instinct you could call the Terror of the Tower. Instincts normally do have survival value. Are we justified in supposing that here we have the great exception?

Let's see.

Yes, I'm going to risk all and make my way in, if I can.

Why?

Why because I must. Because, in spite of the miseries of the Dark Age, a most marvellous thing has happened to me, and I'll be damned if I'll live and die without bothering or daring to look long and steadily at it while I'm able. At this marvellous thing which I suspect is clearly on display inside the Tower and nowhere else.

And exactly what is this marvellous thing that has happened to me?

It is that I've happened!

I need not have done so. Against all the odds (they must be in excess of billions to one) there has arisen from the Abyss of Non-being this particular BEING who can and does now say I AM. Which, they tell me, is none other than the name of the King whose Palace is the Dark Tower, and who is the Source of Being Itself. It would seem that, in claiming to Be, I'm claiming Oneness with Him. This staggering but not absurd claim demands looking into.

And I have other pressing reasons for seeking admittance. I need the protection of a strong Fortress against imminent destruction and death, I need to discover the purpose of my life which (I suspect) is to be found in no Temple outside the Tower. I need the healing which can only be had (it seems) in that *Hotel Dieu,* and above all I desperately need and I long for the sight and the presence of the King over all. In short, I seek entry whatever the risks, whatever the cost.

To my surprise, no moat or drawbridge or portcullis stood between me and the Tower. The only entrance to that gigantic pile turned out to be so small that I had to stoop to pass under its pointed archway. Nor was the door either bolted or guarded. The gentlest push and it swung open, as if I were expected. And, the moment I stepped inside, a fierce blast of wind from within slammed the door violently behind me, with what sounded like a shooting of bolts and a turning of keys. They were telling me there's no going back. I'd come to stay. I was in for it, whatever it might be!

Breathing hard, I found myself standing in a sort of lobby or anteroom, not large but with a high ceiling shrouded in darkness. And the first thing that struck me about the place was its smell. A strong smell which I described to myself as a Stone-Age smell that gets at one's throat. No doubt it was the smell of the rough masonry walls, very cold and gritty to the touch.

A few cautious steps, and, hastily preparing myself for the worst kind of weirdness, I came to another archway, taller than the first and with no door. It gave onto a scene which of all scenes was the least expected. The truly surprising thing about it was its ordinariness, its total lack of surprise. It came as a blow to the solar plexus, that very large gathering of people from the outside world, looking just like and behaving just like they do there—with not a trace of the magic and the mystery that I had anticipated. There they were, hundreds of men and women, young and middle-aged and old, tall and short, handsome and ugly, sloppily and smartly turned out, exhibiting every kind of facial expression from frenetic to serene, moving around freely and forming small and largish groups while a few remained solitary wanderers. The whole scene could have been lifted en bloc from any large party held in the world.

Such was my first impression, standing there in a state of mild shock at the entrance to that spacious hall—a hall much too spacious and well-appointed and well-lit to do duty as the keep or donjon of any ordinary castle.

My second impression was equally shocking, in a very different way. These people weren't talking. They were twittering, as sparrows twitter. Their movements and gestures and facial expressions, in all their ever-changing variety, were the normal sort. Only what came out was (at least in my ears) just twitter—earnest twitter and flippant twitter, excited twitter and calm twitter, high-pitched twitter and low-pitched twitter, loud twitter and whispered twitter—and all of it the same, the same, the same.

I was beginning to feel a bit twittery myself. Was the condition catching? I didn't fancy standing under that pointed arch till kingdom come. Still less, on the other hand, did I fancy stepping out and joining that flock of human sparrows. Not that I was invited. Evidently I was their Invisible Man.

At this juncture another strange thing about the scene struck me— something which, though slower to hit me and less obvious than the twittering, for some obscure reason gave me the shivers. Also it gave me an additional excuse for venturing no further. Nowhere was there any sound of footfall. Soft sandals or hob-nailed boots, shoes gliding or stamping, walking or running—it made no difference. What was it about that floor which muffled and absorbed all the sounds that should have been arising from it? It looked to me much like other floors, solid and safe and smooth and well-polished.

As for the hall itself, it appeared (as I say) much too big to fit into the Tower and its massive stone walls: Was it elastic? Did it have to be that big in order to take in that crowd? In plan it was circular, in height tall and domed, the whole anything but Dark-Age it would seem, but pervaded by that same old smell. The only other thing that I noticed, standing there teetering on the brink, was sundry large pots of yellow flowers scattered at intervals round the perimeter of the hall. Though they were beautiful I couldn't make out their species. Coming from them I picked up the exquisite scent of freesias, localised and feeble in competition with that smell.

I was in a quandary. Should I join those pussy-footed twitterers? In which case I would doubtless be condemning myself for life to their sort of life. Not an encouraging prospect! The alternative, on the other hand—namely, to continue standing on my lonesome under the arch, swaying a little back and forth—seemed just as bad. And the idea of camping in the lobby not only seemed bad but unworkable. For what felt like hours I practised brinkmanship.

And then it happened.

I still swear I made no choice, and that (quite the contrary) some hidden hand pushed me over the brink.

Anyhow I swayed no longer, but stepped onto that peculiar floor.

Only in fact I did nothing of the sort! I stepped through the thing. For me there was absolutely no thing, no floor at all. I shot, head-first, into the Abyss.

The physical shock of that crucial faux pas (or should I say *vrai pas?*), together with the vertigo of that initial loss of balance and foothold, couldn't have been more awful. But, once clear of all support, my terror soon gave place to astonishment and curiosity. My headlong fall could not be faster, nor could the depths it's taking me to appear deeper or more unending—or more fascinating. Am I being gobbled up by the Ogre after all, forever and forever? Are the Ogre of the Tower and its King one and the same Person, the true First Person O-so-singular?

In fact everything down here, everything beneath that treacherous and illusory floor, is visibly the other way up and the diametric opposite of everything above that floor. Up there it's the Aristotelian logic of *A isn't B* that applies, whereas down here it's the Paradoxical logic of *A is B* that applies. Up there the clash of contraries, down here the union of contraries. For instance, up there those other-way-up head-on-top people keep their distance from one another, while down here, though I'm falling away from them, those same people are for me getting no smaller and no less audible, and distance is revealed as the fiction that William Blake said it is. Up there, again, those people are either still or in motion, while down here, though I really am falling fast, I really am perfectly still, just as the Sages and Seers told me I was, and it's the walls of the Abyss that are rushing by—and rushing upwards, at that. Again, up there darkness and light follow each other daily, while down here they come to the same thing, and I'm undecided whether to describe the Bottomless Abyss I'm falling into as the Light that lights up the Light or as the Darkness that extinguishes that Light. My impression is that it's both at once, just as those same Sages and Seers described it. Yet again, up there Being and Consciousness are basic and Nonbeing and Unconsciousness are devalued or dismissed, while down here Nonbeing and Unconsciousness are basic. That's to say: Abysmal. My fall isn't only into the Unknown but into the Unknowable, into what I know with absolute certainty is unknowable.

I go on and on and on falling. Already that awful step onto the floor that was no floor seems ages ago—and no time at all ago. Here, in fact, is yet another abysmal paradox: time is timeless and the timeless is timeful. I look at my wrist-watch, only to discover that its hands and its figures have taken time off!

And of course one of the most obvious differences between the upper world and the nether or abysmal world is that up there everyone's in company, whereas down here I'm on my own, and this plunge into the Abyss is essentially and forever a solitary business.

And yet, of course, the contrary is true, and I am in company all right. And, I'm delighted to say, most illustrious company. Accompanying me in my headlong descent and whispering in my ear, I make out the following—

Hubert Benoit, French psychiatrist: "If you are unhappy it's because you are established in Consciousness instead of the Unconscious."

Nisargadatta Maharaj, like that other Indian sage Ramana Maharshi, insists that our root disease and the cause of all our misery is the illusion "I am this particular person." And its remedy is the realisation "I AM—I am not this or that but pure undifferentiated Being." But this realisation is far from enough. He goes much further. Neatly summing up the whole matter, he announces "I AM shows where to seek but not what to seek. Just have a good look at it… You are the Ground beneath Being, from which all grows," he whispers.

"And this Ground is right now revealing itself to me as ungrounded, as groundless, as the very Absence of any ground whatever," I whisper back.

Eugen Herrigel, German philosopher and Benoit's contemporary, is specially helpful: "All things, seen from their Origin, are equal, have an absolute value. Their Origin or Ground can be perceived only through them. You see, with absolute certainty, that things are by virtue of what they are not. To the degree that their formless Origin is inaccessible and inconceivable, things in their concrete form become more accessible. Bathed in the light of their Origin, they themselves are illuminated."

I do so agree. Down here I'm finding those beautiful yellow flowers *more* beautiful, and even *more* deliciously scented, than when I first saw them from the archway. As for the twitterers milling around in their midst, none is really ugly or dispensable, and their twittering is beginning to resemble a kind of music.

Herrigel went to Japan from the West, while D.T. Suzuki came to the West from Japan, bringing Zen: "How rich," he exclaims, "is the inward life of the man of Zen, because it is in direct communication with the great Unconscious… This unknown, once recognised, enters into ordinary consciousness and puts in good order all the complexities that have been tormenting us to greater or less degrees… As soon as it is recognised that consciousness comes out of something which, though not known in the way relative things are known, is intimately related to us, we are relieved of every form of tension and are thoroughly at rest and at peace with ourselves and with the world generally."

Very different in her language but very similar in her logic—paradoxical logic—is that remarkable lady, the Blessed Angela of Foligno. She confesses: "I put all my hope in a secret good, which I apprehend in a great darkness. All creatures filled with God, the divine power and will—all is inferior to this most hidden good. Those other things bring delight, but this vision of God in darkness brings no smile to the lips, no devotion or fervour to the soul… Yet all the countless and unspeakable words and favours of God to me fall so far short of this vision of God in darkness that I put no trust in them at all."

"Yes," I reply. "The God up there was for seeking in the light and maybe finding in the light. But the God down here is for seeking in the darkness and certainly losing in the darkness. And the funny thing and the beautiful thing is that this loss of Him and parting from Him (and this alone) is the true finding of Him and union with Him. It sounds silly, and feels right—absolutely right. The wisdom of God is foolishness to men."

All of which is confirmed, with unparalleled conviction and eloquence, by the Blessed Jan van Ruysbroeck. He speaks to me of "the uncomprehended Light, wayless and fathomless." If we could know and comprehend it, it would fall into mode and measure, and this could never satisfy us. Only because it is inaccessible and abysmal is this "wild darkness of the Godhead" our sure refuge.

And, as further evidence that God-talk and Zen-talk can be perfectly compatible, here is the matchless Meister Eckhart: "The end is the mystery of the darkness of the eternal Godhead, and it is unknown and never will be known... God dwells therein unknown to Himself... He is a not-God, a not-mind, neither a person nor an image. Sink eternally from something to nothing in Him." And Eckhart's disciple Tauler speaks of "the fathomless Abyss, bottomless and floating in itself, which is much more God's dwelling than Heaven or man is."

"And much more, "I add, "than the Dark Tower is."

But full marks for brevity and punch to Rumi, the Persian Sufi poet and sage: "A thing which is not to be found—that is my goal."

My unending fall into the dark Abyss consists of unending surprises. But amongst them all is the one that stands out starkly, that please God I shall never begin to get used to. It is this. The God whose Palace is the Dark Tower, but whose Home is the Abyss beneath the Tower, dwells therein *unknown to Himself, and He will forever remain unknown and unknowable.* So says Meister Eckhart. And so says Hui Hai, alias The Great Pearl, one of the most notable Zen (or rather Ch'an) masters of the T'ang Dynasty. *"Prajna* (The Perfection of Wisdom, our Buddha Nature) is unconscious, but facing the yellow flowers it functions." And I say the same, facing as I do those beautiful and sweet-scented yellow flowers, so tastefully arranged up there around the perimeter of the great hall.

How grateful I am for the hidden hand—it was surely His hand—that pushed me over the brink into His very own unattainable depths!

PART TWO

Here are the relevant extracts from my 2002 diary:

Tuesday, April 2 I completed the story of the Dark Tower, which is Part One of this chapter. There it was, spelled out on my computer, and it hasn't been changed since then.

Thursday, April 4 It was read by Jacinta Wright, a friend who visited us that day.

Friday, April 5 My wife Catherine and I drove from Suffolk to Winchester, where we participated in a weekend conference of some two hundred people.

Sunday, April 7 After successfully descending some thirty steps from the dining hall to the conference hall, I stopped briefly at its entrance. Then I stepped onto the floor that wasn't there, and fell headlong. In fact, failing to see this last step, I fell and broke my hip.

Sunday, April 21 Here am I, in Winchester and Eastleigh Hospital, learning to walk on my reconstructed hip.

Twice in one week I have stepped onto a floor that wasn't there! On the first (and pseudo-fictional) occasion, I found it fairly easy to thank God for pushing me into His bottomless abyss. On the second and all-too-realistic occasion I'm finding it harder to thank Him— and even more necessary.

To be stuck here in this ward for a fortnight surely ranks as a most dreary experience. In fact John, the patient in the opposite bed, having his broken leg in traction, is enduring some five weeks of what he describes as an agony of boredom. It may be an agony of boredom approaching at times the dreadful state of *accidie* or torpor which used to be reckoned one of the Seven Deadly Sins.

Here, by the grace of God, it's rather different. It's not that I'm evading or escaping boredom, but, on the contrary, that I'm wallowing in it, falling continually into its unplumbed depths. With the surprising result that not for a second have I been bored since arriving here. Long live Paradox!

And thanks be to God for the second push. For His lovingkindness (not unmixed with humour) in arranging that what he has to teach me about falling into Him is told twice over. He tells these things at least twice to slow learners, hopefully doubling their impact. I'm lost in admiration of the ways he has of rubbing in the message.

22. THERE, BUT FOR THE GRACE OF GOD, GO I

It was the six o'clock news on the TV.

The suffering on that face was terrible. Yes, I know: the thing he had done was terrible too. His victim suffered appallingly. But, thank god, the agony was brief. And now I can't help thinking of the villain's agony, spread out probably over several decades. Several decades of excruciating torture, beginning with those furious crowds surrounding the prison that would lynch him if they could, and followed by the permanent loathing from the fellow prisoners he has to be protected from! The psychiatric experts have found him sufficiently sane to stand trial. No wonder there are dark shadows under his eyes, and his hair is whiter than it was when we saw him a week or two ago. No wonder he stumbled as he left the court.

I'm not saying that society and its laws could or should do anything different to him than this. All the same, I cannot forget he is my brother. At his Centre is the light that lights *everyone* who comes into the world, and at Root, I am him. No way can I wash my hands of this tortured soul. I *take on* his awful guilt and pain. But *taking it away* is a very different thing. That is the business not of me but of the Christ who dwells in me. Of course I don't know whether one day he will come around to that supernal realization. I very much doubt it. But while there's life there's hope.

Meantime there's work be done on myself in this matter. "There, but for the grace of God, go I." I say this in all sincerity. Given the parentage and upbringing of that poor man, given his genes and chromosomes and all that hereditary conditioning, given his temperament as it was handed to him at birth, *would I have behaved any differently?* The answer is NO, NO, NO! I would have done exactly what he did. In fact I have to say, instead of "There, but for the grace of God, go I", "There go I", simply and in any case.

This is the way of the Christ in me, the way of the Cross, which I have slowly come to realise is the way of the Reality and the Power that underlies the world. Sometimes in the course of my work over the past half century, people have asked me what my recipe is for getting rid of pain: and I have to say to them that I had no recipe. That, on the contrary, that my recipe was for taking on pain, the pain of the world, which includes of course the pain of that execrated prisoner in the dock.

That eminent saint and sage Johann Tauler of Strasbourg, had lots of profound things to say about the necessity for pain. For example, "A man once thought that God drew some men by pleasant paths, while others were drawn by the path of pain. Our Lord answered him thus: What do you think can be pleasanter or nobler than to be made most like Me, that is by suffering? To whom was even offered such a troubled life as to Me? And in whom can I better work in accordance with My true nobility than in those who are most like Me? They are the men who suffer... Learn that My divine nature never worked so nobly in human nature as by suffering; and because suffering is so efficacious it is sent out of great love. I understand the weakness of human nature at all times, and out of love and righteousness I lay no heavier load than man can bear. The crown must be firmly pressed down that is to bud and blossom in the Eternal Presence of My Heavenly Father. He who desires to be immersed in the fathomless sea of My Godhead must also be deeply immersed in the sea of bitter sorrow. I am exalted far above all things and work supernatural and wonderful works in Myself. Thus the deeper and more supernaturally a man crushes himself beneath all things the more supernaturally will he be drawn above all things." (Tauler, Sermon on St. Paul, *The Inner Way*, London 1909. p. 114)

At this juncture, I see you saying something like this to me: "You are evidently some kind of Christian. Well, I'm not a Christian. Along with growing numbers in the West, I find that Christianity requires me to believe all sorts of incredible things, or to pretend that I believe them. This I cannot do."

To which I reply like this. I don't believe any of those impossible things either and many Christians would hotly deny that I am any sort of Christian. This doesn't bother me in the slightest, nor, as I see it, does it bother my God who so graciously takes up residence in me. And I do suggest to you that humility in the face of the data, of what's clearly given, is of much higher value in the spiritual life than blind faith in the incredible. God Himself values the truth above even the most sacrosanct of fictions. It cost Him death on the Cross.

Of course, I grant you that the story of the Cross is a shocking and terrible story, but I'm convinced it's the true one. To be is to be like that. As I see it, the explanation (in so far as an explanation of this mystery of mysteries is possible) runs like this. The creation of the world cost the Creator dear. Very dear indeed. Sublime love and joy were to be had, but only at the cost of His own Crucifixion.

It's no use replying that for God all things are possible, and that He could have made man sinless and happy. That was impossible even for Him.

Why?

For the simple reason that a creature who is perforce innocent and incapable of sin is no man but rather a nice sort of animal. Freedom, which includes freedom to be a Hitler or an Ivan the Terrible or a Nero, is an essential ingredient of human nature. You could say that, though it's an exceedingly blessed nature to be given, it's a mixed blessing, and it comes with a high price tag attached. The freedom to choose the evil alternative instead of the good alternative is never quite absent from any sane human being.

I can hear you objecting that I have just been saying that the man in the dock, accused of that terrible crime, was the slave and victim of his many-sided conditioning, and was not free to do other than he did.

Well, I admit the inconsistency, and reply as follows. Human nature is a mass and a mess of contradictions, a mystery compounded of insoluble mysteries. All of us, sinners and saints, are profoundly conditioned, and even more profoundly relieved of and set free from that conditioning by God our Saviour. I doubt whether God himself understands human nature through and through. Instead He has a more radical alternative. He takes it on, and is crucified, and offers us salvation instead of explanation. In taking on human nature at Calvary, He not only takes on our guilt and misery, but, along with all that, its built-in nonsenses. I don't say He makes sense of them, but that He transcends them.

Let me put it this way. He has set us free, and He is our freedom. Apart from Him (as if anyone or anything could be apart from Him!) we are all of us, the holiest of saints and the most depraved of sinners and all between, conditioned through and through, the most abject of slaves, chained hand and foot, programmed down to the last tremor. Only He who is our Being is unconditioned, and when He sets us free He does so in the only way that's possible. He offers us union with Him. He alone is the great De-conditioner. He is our Saviour, and his salvation is none other than His very own residence at our Centre, His lodging—the whole of Him, nothing missing—in our very heart. And, as I have so often said, he or she in whom God dwells has a good lodger.

Nor does He fail to show up there very clearly, displaying with all possible brilliance the characteristics we recognise Him by— Boundlessness, No-thingness, Unlimited Receptivity, Timelessness and Imperishability, Wide-awakeness, His Immense Single Eye with its awesome Powers of Creation and Destruction, His Immobility along with its Power to Move the World. And so on. The list is long and could scarcely be more impressive. Q.E.D. Q.E.D.

So, back to our prisoner in the dock. His salvation, exactly like yours and mine, his escape from the hell of his conditioning, is conscious union with his Source. With all my heart I pray that one day, sooner rather than later, his pain will push him into making that leap.

Meanwhile, let me never forget that at Root I am him.

23. THE OTHER CHEEK

The claim that a man must die to the worldly world and all its notions, if he is to live "the life that is life indeed", is as obvious throughout the New Testament as in the Gospels... The Church of Christ has dared absolutely to reverse the methods of its Master. *Bishop Gore*

Besides being an eminent churchman, Charles Gore (1853-1930) was a deeply committed and gifted disciple of Jesus Christ. Yet he says a shocking thing. God knows what a visitor from outer space would make of it, how astonished he would be at the agelong and near-universal contradiction and double-think that the bishop describes. And surely the most shocking thing about it is that we aren't shocked, that we take it for granted, that we have it for breakfast and dinner and tea, that we take it in our stride. Apart from the occasional maverick like Bishop Gore, the Sermon on the Mount is so much holy water on the ecclesiastical duck's back, on all our ducks' backs.

I find it difficult to think of a more puzzling segment of human history. Here's the adored founder of one of the world's major religions, laying down precisely and for all time the way his followers must live if they are to be his followers and not his enemies. And here are these followers—millions and millions of them, including all manner of holy saints and brilliant theologians and inspired poets—at once insisting on and dismissing off-hand their Master's maxims as quite impracticable. Saying one thing and casually doing its opposite. For two thousand years this anomaly of anomalies has been going on, almost without trace of the moral embarrassment the Early Christians suffered from.

In this chapter let's try to ferret out if we can what sense underlies this nonsense, this built-in contradiction. It's conceivable that our huge company of hypocrites and betrayers of their Master, looked at from another level or another angle, will turn out to be nothing of the sort, and we shall find a way of making honest men and women of them.

But first let's examine in a little more detail the discrepancy between the Master's guidelines for living and his disciples' guidelines for living.

If my neighbour encloses a strip of my land, do I offer him an additional strip? Or do I ring up my solicitor?

If the repairs to my roof cost twice what they should, do I pay up happily? Or do I insist on a big reduction?

If a careless driver in a car-park backs into my radiator, do I pay for the repairs to both the cars? Or do I make him pay?

If someone publicly denounces my life's work as confused, trivial, fraudulent, or plain silly, do I thank him for his help in detaching me from my work and its results? And, if I happen to meet him, am I likely to embrace him? Or do I lose no opportunity of vigorously defending myself?

If a terrorist, having already killed a number of my fellow-countrymen, threatens to go on doing so, what is my reaction? Do

I send out to him silent messages of understanding, reconciliation, forgiveness, compassion, and love? Or of loathing? Do I support my country's punitive measures, or do I condemn them rather than him?

And so on and on...

Of course there have been a lot of attempts down the centuries, both in theory and in practice, to bridge this moral gap. Communism, intent on abolishing private property and privilege, has been tried out again and again in its many varieties, from the earliest Christian community to all sorts of New-World utopias, to Leninism and Stalinism and Pol-Potism. Tried out, at best, without lasting success, and at worst with results that are quite devilish. Attempt to build a heaven on earth, and you risk building hell.

The moral chasm yawns as wide as ever. Is it unbridgeable? Must we go on like this? Could the main reason for our current spate of problems be our failure to build the flimsiest of bridges over the chasm? Is there no healing for this dreadful wound? That's the question we are addressing here.

Judging by results to date, to go on trying to build a bridge along the old lines is inviting failure. A new and unorthodox design—perhaps a flagrantly unorthodox design—is called for. The time has come, at the close of this unproductive two-thousand-year trial period, to try building a radically new kind of bridge between Christ and Christendom.

What follows is a rough sketch rather than a blueprint of that bridge as I see it.

For a start let's recognise that there's no risk of a real Utopia breaking out. The divine perfection that we humans are invited to share in doesn't lie at the human level. Far from it. No, what we are seeking here on Earth isn't the perfecting but the radical amelioration of mankind, based on what we SEE we are.

Let me explain. The proper lifestyle of a bird in the air is determined through and through by its winged and feathered physique. The proper lifestyle of a fish in the sea is determined through and through by its finned and scaly physique. In much the same way the proper lifestyle of man on Earth is determined through and through by his very peculiar physique. We shall presently be testing the hypothesis that we are in grievous trouble because our physique and our lifestyle don't match. Because, in other words, we fall far short of our physical potential. Yes, I'm very serious about this adjective. In fact, our initial reliance on the physical instead of the mental and spiritual is what's novel in our approach—an approach from the bottom up, so to say. And I mean the physical as it's clearly on display, cleansed as far as possible of imaginative and conceptual distortion and elaboration. For a change we are going to see what happens when we go by what we see we see, instead of what we think we see and what we're told we see.

It's just as if our body were trying to tell us what has gone wrong with our mind, and showing how to put it right.

This means that both of us will now have to carry out an experiment.

Throughout the following experiment I speak for myself, not you. My hope, of course, is that what I discover about me resembles what you discover about you. But I don't insist on it. What you are for you is for you and you alone to settle. I'm literally in no position to tell you.

It may be that you have done this experiment before, perhaps many times. For this I make no apology. Quite the reverse. All our experiments have a dual purpose. They are procedures for uncovering new facts and exercises for practising those facts, for building them into our everyday lives, and the more we conscientiously repeat them the better. I must have carried out this particular experiment many hundreds of times, and every time feels like the first time. And please remember that the question it addresses is crucial.

I'm asking you to draw your body (your clothed body, of course), to draw what's clearly on show, no more and no less. It's simply a matter of outlining on paper or card the opaque, textured, and coloured shapes that make up the currently visible parts of your human body.

To see it all the way up you must of course use your mirror—the full-length one.

Please draw what you see there in the mirror as best you can. And I'll draw what I see in my mirror. [1]

---

1 A useful but not so valuable alternative to drawing yourself (not so valuable because not so active and challenging) is that you photograph yourself in the mirror. Photograph, that's to say, what you find of yourself in your camera's viewfinder, no more and no less, while remembering that your camera is far less liable to distort and superimpose things on it than you are.

Well, here's my effort. I'll assume that our two pictures turn out much the same.

So far, so good. But now you have to ask yourself, and I have to ask myself, the First Big Question—WHERE AM I?

Are you over there on the far side of your mirror, or are you here on the near side, a yard or so closer than him or her? Which of these two bodies tickles, and senses the pressure of your bottom on the chair, and feels tired or sprightly?

If you agree that the obvious answer is that you belong on the near side of your mirror, I have to put to you and to myself the Second Big Question—IS THE BODY THIS SIDE OF THE MIRROR VISIBLY THE SAME AS THE BODY THAT SIDE, EXCEPT THAT IT'S THE OTHER WAY ROUND?

To make sure we get the right answer a second drawing (or photograph) is called for. Let both of us now add, underneath the portrait of the one on the far side of the mirror, our portrait of the one this side of it, drawing (or photographing) only what we see of ourself.

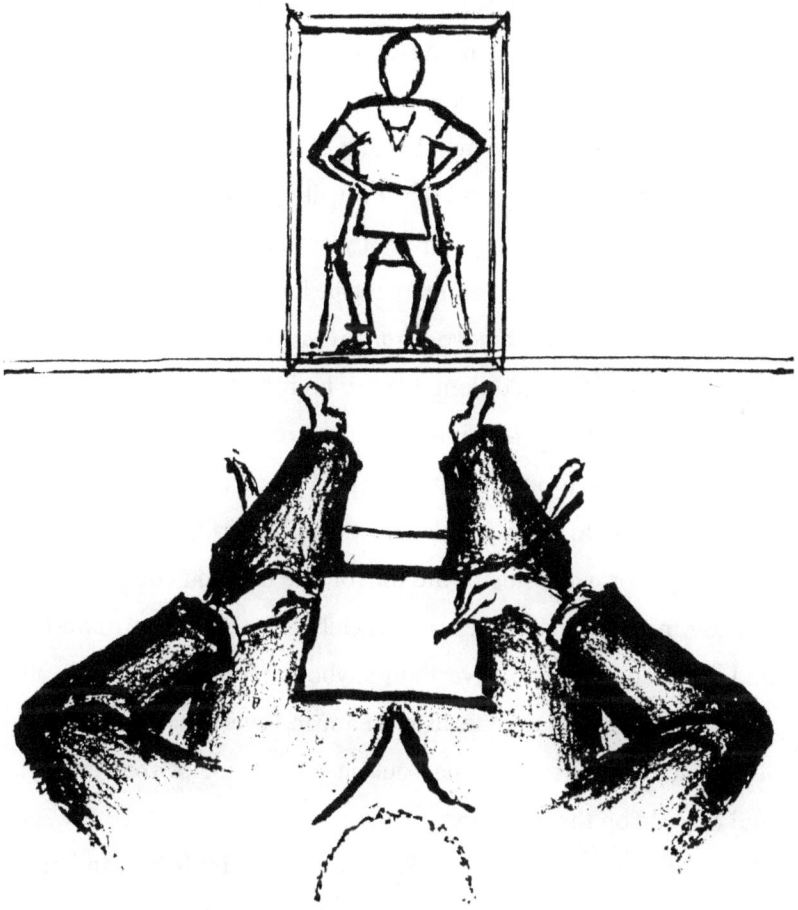

Now if (allowing for our different styles of draughtsmanship) you get what I get, then I submit for your agreement the following observations:

(1) Like me, you have and you need two very different kinds of human body, and here are some of their differences—

(2) The body on the near side of the glass is the one you are in, while the body on the far side of the glass is the one you have. This one

is what you are for you, while that one is what you are for others, and they don't match. On the other hand they are profoundly interdependent in all sorts of ways.

(3) That body settles your membership of the human race and your separate human identity, and that's why it figures in your passport, while this one leaves the question of your true identity wide open. Pending our observations about that true identity, you can certainly announce to the world that you aren't what you look like.

(4) In fact you see, ranged alongside that body in the mirror, a varying number of similar (but less shiny) specimens of the human race. Over there you are visibly one of millions, a paid-up member of the human club and subject to its rules and regulations, its penalties and rewards.

(5) The one on your side of the mirror, the one you coincide with and are in, is a member of no such club. Search diligently and far and wide, and you will never find anybody resembling you. In all the universe you are unique. Just as I am and everyone else is at this level. Such paradoxes are ruled out on the far side of your mirror, and ruled in on the near side.

(6) Among the many visible differences between this human body and that human body (or, if you prefer, between the one you are in and the one you have) are the following:

That body, like all those others, is visibly headed. This unique one is visibly beheaded. It terminates in a semicircular Frontier that stretches from your left shoulder to your right shoulder. To make sure of this try tracing, with your forefinger touching your shirt or blouse, the line where your fingernail disappears.

You could say that the body you have on the far side of your mirror lives an imaginary or unreal or pseudo-life, while the body you are on this side lives a real and very lively life. But it's not nearly so simple as that. Up to the Frontier that's the way it is, but beyond the Frontier it's very different. Here you vanish without trace in favour of the one you are facing. On this side of your mirror is the place where opposites meet and become one, and life and death are revealed as the two sides of a coin.

The awesome fact is that beyond the Frontier, whether you admit it or not, you die for the other. But this isn't enough. If you want to taste real joy you will also live for him on the lively side of the Frontier.

At this point I seem to hear you saying: "That's a very different sort of death from the one I'm familiar with."

I heartily agree. It's real death. Unlike the sort the undertaker undertakes, the sort that leaves a lot of matter to be disposed of, there's nothing whatever left of you. Beyond the Frontier you really do make way for him or her absolutely. No special credit to you. You are built like that. What I'm proposing is that you and I should wake up to the fact, that we should consciously live the way we really are this side of our mirrors.

The practical question we must now ask is this. Just how far does our conscious shift from a one-body life to a two-body life promise to help you and me to shift to a two-morality life, in which these two contrasting moralities are reconciled as thoroughly as these two bodies already are.

To get some idea of how this reconciliation works out, let's go back to the case of the neighbour who invaded a strip of your garden.

What do you do?

You write him a polite but firm letter, but get no reply. You phone him asking for an explanation, without response. But you do succeed in arranging a meeting.

Throughout that meeting you clearly see what meets what. In fact you see that it's not really a meeting at all, and that he hasn't only invaded your garden but you. You notice that you can't take in his face without taking leave of yours, that beyond the Frontier you have nothing to keep him out with, that you really do die the deepest of deaths for him.

And it's impossible to do more for him than that. Which surely reduces your territorial dispute to triviality and not worth a moment's fussing about.

Of course there's no predicting what he will do. Maybe at some level your conscious disappearance in his favour will get across to him, with the result that he hands back the stolen land. But even if he doesn't, and he hangs on to it, the issue is reduced to its proper proportions, and you leave him in possession...

"This way," I hear you saying, "all sorts of people are going to take advantage of me."

Well, I'm sure that you'll find it's an immeasurably happier policy, and in the long run much more practical, than being taken disadvantage of. But don't believe me. Try it out and see. See and try it out. The prospects are good, but we can't be certain of results. Jesus

Christ said he came to show us the truth that sets us free. And the price of freedom is unpredictability.

"That's all very well," you tell me, "but what about the terrorist? How much effect are my messages of forgiveness and reconciliation likely to have on him?"

Of course we just don't know. But let's remember that Jesus Christ describes his disciples as the salt of the earth and the light of the world, in the absence of which the world will surely make straight for hell.

There's no substitute for the patient practice of life and death this side of our mirror. Practice and trust, as we ask what's impossible for the One that not only achieves the hyper-miracle of Self-origination but offers you and me the most intimate union with the Self-originator. Let's take up that offer, and see what happens.

At this point you may tell me that there's no real call for our newfangled way Home to our True Nature, and that it adds nothing to the way that seers and sages have been taking down the centuries.

I don't see it as adding anything essential, but rather as making it available. Our aim here is that what used to be called the Beatific Vision (alias conscious union with our Source) which used to be the privilege of very few, very gifted men and women living very unnatural lives apart from the world, should become available to us ordinary people living ordinary lives in the world. That it should indeed become the Norm or Standard, falling short of which we are regarded as cases of arrested development. That it should no longer be perceived as a rare achievement but as what it really is—our Natural

State, uniquely shareable, and in perfect accord with the findings of modern science. Surely this is none other than the re-discovery of the obvious, and the old, old story which richly deserves to be newly told.

All good stories involve warfare. Jesus Christ avoided a premature and simplistic unity. He came wielding a sword, the sharp sword that discriminates between the things that are Caesar's and the things that are God's, between the kingdom of this world and the kingdom of heaven. He was a dualist before he was a monist, a warrior before he was a peacemaker.

And now, inspired by him, we come wielding a sword from the same armoury—the sharp-edged mirror-sword that discriminates between what we look like and what we are, between the body we live with and the body we live in, between that distant apology for life and this real life and death. And so at last we learn to live simultaneously in his world and our world without hypocrisy and double-think, and to appreciate just how realistic and how workable that Sermon of his is.

BE WHAT YOU ARE

BOTH SIDES OF THE GLASS

AND BOTH SIDES OF THE FRONTIER

24. EFFING THE INEFFABLE—MYSTICISM IN REVERSE

Until a few days ago I thought that my job—the purpose and meaning of my life—was to cultivate and disseminate a kind of mysticism. A very peculiar kind, to be sure, but still coming under that heading. I imagined I was a dyed-in-the-wool mystic.

How wrong I was!

Now, at long last, I see that my job has all along been to put mysticism in reverse, to stand it on its head, to contradict it in all respects, as I shall presently explain.

But first let me say how understandable was the notion that I was a mystic and no opponent of mysticism. The books I loved to read, and still love to read, are by the great mystics, including Rumi, Meister Eckhart, John Tauler and Ruysbroeck; no wonder other people no less than myself regarded me as a mystic, albeit a peculiar sort of mystic. And still from time to time I look back with delight upon the great mystical experiences of my life, and I would be thrilled to be granted one or two more before I die.

To give you some idea of those experiences, here, in brief, are two of them. At the age of (I think) eleven I read, in Dickens' *Tale of Two Cities,* the story of a man who loved a woman so dearly that he gave his life for the man she loved, for his rival. For several hours after reading this story I looked out on an utterly transformed world. The very bricks of the town were heavenly. The other instance I call to mind occurred only ten years ago, in a beautiful sunlit and fragrant meadow in the south of France. A circle dance of expert dancers with flowing hair and garments was in progress, accompanied by enchanting zither music. Why I was bowled over with love and joy for hours and hours I can't tell you. It was a mystical experience all right.

All the same, it's a fact that my life's work has been and still is to up-end mysticism, to set it in reverse. In this sense I'm an antimystic. As I shall now try to explain.

Effing the ineffable

You will have seen how easily I can describe to you the scenery and circumstances of a mystical occasion. What I can't begin to convey to you is the ecstasy, the thrill, the transformation of the world that arose from the scenery and the circumstances of that occasion. All that is truly ineffable, absolutely indescribable.

My business is to point out and eff the ineffable. Thus I ask you to use your right forefinger to point to what you are looking out of, to what you see you are right here at your Centre. And you tell me that what you see is empty space, nothing at all. But you add that this empty space isn't just empty. It's empty for filling with whatever happens to be on offer, which varies from your hands and feet to a sky of a million stars. The Nothing that you see you are explodes into Everything.

Now one of the peculiar things about this inseeing is that, thanks to the pointing finger, this Nothingness-Allness is perfectly obvious. Throughout the past half century or so I have not come across anyone who saw this partially or with effort, or shrouded in some sort of mist.

How can one see an absence, an absence of anything to see? You may well ask.

Very easily, I reply. We do just that all the time. For instance, seeing the absence of a salt-cellar on the dining table, you hasten to remedy the lack. Seeing the absence of your child at the breakfast table, you go and warn him that he will be late for school. Seeing the absence of carrots and parsnips in your pantry, you go and buy some. Yes of course, the absence of things is at least as obvious as their presence, and the permanent absence of all things at your Core couldn't be more obvious, more effable, once you know where to look. How different is this experience from a mystical experience, which of all experiences is the least obvious, the most rare and hidden and ineffable!

And of course, along with the blazing obviousness of this unmystical vision, goes its shareability, its commonness, its sameness for all who enjoy it. No other experience is so unifying. So much so that those who share it often say to one another: Here I am you! How different, again, from the mystical vision, which is essentially private and (at least in the feel of it, if not in its substance) quite unique. Mysticism holds people apart. Unmysticism brings them together, with the greatest of ease.

At this point I can hear some of my readers asking which of the two antithetical experiences is the profounder. Surely, they feel, the more difficult and rare mystical experience runs deeper than the all-too-common and commonplace and cheap unmystical experience.

My answer to this very reasonable objection runs like this. Mystical experiences are hot, while unmystical ones are cool. If mystical experiences can be ranked in any order of importance, the more ecstatic and overwhelming they are the higher they rank. But this heat and intensity of feeling is NOT a reliable guide to depth, to the truth of what is revealed. The ecstasy I enjoyed while watching those circle-dancers, and for some time afterwards, was marvellous, but by itself brought me no nearer to What I am Where I am, to my Root. It takes my antimystical, ordinary, natural, common-or-garden experience of my Nothingness-Everythingness to do that. In fact it's notorious that some very genuine mystical experiences have no spiritual or metaphysical content at all. For example, my very first visit to the cinema, at the tender age of twenty-one (to see the German war film *All Quiet on the Western Front*) was a mystical experience that transmogrified my London for days, but it did nothing to bring me any nearer to my true Identity at Root. That came ten years later, and it was as cool and natural and refreshing as the clear air of the morning. This antimystical experience is the one that invariably runs deep, the mystical experience may or may not do so.

Maybe you are still not satisfied. The best cases of mystical experience (I can hear you saying) are experiences of union with God, with the Kingdom and the Power and the Glory that underlie the world, with the Great Mystery of Being. Where in the antimystical experience can one find any Divinity to compare with this?

Well, I have to admit that I can't find in the New Testament or the Old Testament, or in any of the great scriptures of the world, or in the writings of the great majority of the mystics belonging to the great traditions, any trace of the God I find here at my Centre. This God does the "impossible" thing. He is the Self-originating One, the One who gets around to creating Himself before He was around to do so, the One who ought not be, yet is. Now this God, far, far more than the God-that-has-to-be of the scripture, I find to be absolutely adorable. He bowls me over. And to find Him at my very heart—what a wonder and a joy that is!

I don't say, mind you, that all the friends with whom I share the antimystical experience have discovered this "impossible" God. But at least they are well on the way to doing so. It comes naturally when it comes, and is altogether different from the mystic's traditional God, the God-who-must-be.

This huge difference may account for the fact that whereas a mystic needs to belong to one or another of the great religions—Advaita Vedanta, Theravada Buddhism, Mahayana Buddhism, Orthodox or Catholic or Protestant Christianity, Islam of the Sufi or some other variety—an antimystic is under no such obligation. He's a free-thinker. All traditions belong to him, he belongs to none.

But you are far from satisfied. Mysticism produces great saints, you tell me, and ask what saints antimysticism produces, or is ever likely to produce. How could such a cheap, give-away, easy-as-winking, debilitating experience do more than come up with dirt-cheap goods? In short, you refuse to believe that what's truly valuable doesn't have to be worked for and agonized for. One may even have to give one's life for it.

With almost all of this objection I heartily agree. Let me explain why.

Yes of course, nothing could be easier than to see the Emptiness here at my Centre when my finger points it out to me. And nothing could be harder than to see it and consciously to live from it all the while, in all the circumstances of daily life. Occasionally to point in to the truth is the very beginning of our spiritual life, which amounts to very little if we are content with just that. To be effective in our own life and to achieve any worthwhile and lasting result in the world, assiduous practice is indispensable—practice till the new habit of uninterrupted seeing into one's Nature is established, and one's trust in leaning back upon that Nature takes over one's life. No doubt each act of inseeing and trusting is pretty easy, it's keeping them going in times of stress and strain that's so difficult and challenging.

Of course you are right when you say that our antimysticism has produced no saints. But I say: Give it time, and there's no reason why it should not do so.

As for your notion that our antimysticism is debilitating, that it lets us off working for the welfare of our suffering brothers and sisters, nothing could be further from the truth. To the extent to which this experience is pursued it fits and energises us for precisely this work. I have friends who live for this purpose, and would die for it.

And the concluding paradox is this. My antimysticism is in the end promystical. I'm not less but more a mystic because my life's work has been to contradict mysticism!

It's as if I must go to the loo before ever ever eating. In God even dirt's holy.

As Martin Buber finely says: "One should hallow all that one does in one's natural life."

25. I AM

When I listen to what I'm saying I find that two quite contrary things are going on.

On the one hand, what I say misleads me disastrously. For example, when I say (excusing myself when I'm caught with my hand in the till) "after all, I'm only human," I'm talking absolute unmitigated balderdash. Nothing could be further from the truth. What am I without my ingredients—cells, molecules, atoms and so on?—or without my environment so-called, such as Mankind, and Earth, and the life on Earth, the Sun and its light and energy, and so on? Without the whole blessed Hierarchy?

On the other hand, when I listen carefully to what I'm saying, it can and does very often give expression to profound truths that are hidden from me, and that I desperately need to become aware of. It's as if Something or Someone deep and precious in me is struggling to get out. This chapter is about that mysterious Something, and about my very often speaking far wiser than I know.

I'm talking for myself here because I have to, but of course I very much hope it's ringing a resounding peal of bells in you.

Here are some of the many instances—each independent of the others, please note—of your deepest but much overlooked wisdom.

You ask me *how I am*. Which, read one way, is just about the most challenging and profound question you could possibly ask me. And which, read the other way, is just about the least challenging and most shallow question you could ask me—and it calls for and gets the answer that I am well, or poorly, thank you very much, as the case may be.

Or you ask me whether *I am in pain*. Which, read one way, calls for the stout assertion that, on the contrary, I am in nothing, and all things are in me. And which, read the other way, calls for the easiest and most superficial reply that I'm pretty comfortable at the moment, thank you kindly.

In point of fact I'm very, very frequently being asked, or asking myself, such questions about myself as What am I up to? What am I doing tomorrow? What am I thinking about? Where am I more comfortable, in this chair or in that chair? And so on and on. And of course all these questions have two wildly contrasting kinds of answer. The key to that contrast isn't hard to spot. It consists in the fact that, throughout all such questioning, the Asker stays the same, never varying by a hair's breadth, while the question asked varies endlessly. The all-too-easy and superficial kind of reply attends only to the ever-changing question and doesn't bother with the never-changing Asker who is the Source of all questions and answers, their Root and Origin. Alas the switch over from asked to Asker is at present extremely rare. No wonder the world is in such a mess!

Well, how far have I got in this inquiry? Let me take stock.

I'm telling myself all the time, whether I listen to myself or not, that I AM, that truly I AM THE ONE WHO IS, the One who performs the "impossible" miracle of Self-Origination. Which is surely the most marvellous piece of good news imaginable. I ought to be dancing and throwing my hat in the air with joy. Why am I not doing so?

Perhaps the reason is this. Every human being of the past and present and future is fully set up to say what I'm saying and make exactly the same awesome discovery about himself or herself, and I can't imagine how many billions they number. I know, of course, that only a minute proportion of them has so far awakened to the truth, but at least the potential is there. Which it seems makes nonsense of my claim to identity here with the One Unique I AM. Surely it dilutes that claim from full strength to weaker than dishwater.

Let me try to deal with this most reasonable and powerful of objections.

Am I suggesting that the One I AM is an absurd fiction, because (supposing it ever existed) it has manifestly spawned countless I AMs? That because every one of them is an I AM and fully authorised, along with me, to announce its own particular I AMness, the presence of the Unique One at my Centre is impossible?

Well, I don't know about you, but for me this wholesale dispersion of BEING or ISness or the I AM and seeming destruction of any central I AMness of my own, is complete. Apparently the very idea that this unique I AM is in any sense at my Centre is shown up as absurd and quite unbelievable egotism. It challenges me to look for a much more credible solution to my problem. The following is the one I'm coming up with.

The pseudo-I-AMness that all of us humans can claim and do claim as separate individuals is altogether secondary and derivative and downstream of the Indivisible One Who, properly speaking, alone IS. It is His gracious gift which is designed to start us off on our search for the perfectly indivisible One that underlies all creation. And if and when we do get on with and succeed in that search, we shall each of us clearly recognise that he or she (as such) is infinitely remote from the One. And that, in so far as you or I arrive at unity with that One, we disappear without trace and the One takes over. The price of His total Presence at our Centre is our total absence.

All right I say, but I'm left with the problem of my attitude to the billions of those whose claim to oneness with the One is equal to my claim. My delighted consent to vanishing in His favour doesn't let me off my dealings with them. They become my problem.

Well, I have to acknowledge that the One that I have disappeared into here is every one of those myriads, and that in becoming One with the One I'm one with them all. And that His presence here therefore implies and includes their presence here. Yes, the lot! So, if somehow I deny this fact, off He goes like a shot!

This can only mean that I have to take in and to take on every one of them, for the simple reason that I do so already! I don't mean that I take on the parts that I like, and reject the rest. No, I have to take on board the pain and guilt of all, which is exactly the theme of this book. I have arrived at this conclusion by a different road, but it is a fast trunk road.

What I suspect it does add, what's unique, if not indispensable, about this trunk road, is this:

Travelling home by this road I become quite sure, first, of the absolute necessity of saving all beings from suffering and guilt, and secondly, of the absolute truth of the fact that I'm able to do so only by virtue of the fact that the start of the One here is the end of Douglas here. I'm always in danger (owing to an ingrained and hard-to-exorcise habit) of putting that little human at the Centre of my life and Being. After forty years or so of chucking him out, he's still lying in wait, and terribly good at creeping back here.

This main trunk road helps me marvellously to go on chucking. I pack him off along that broad two-directional highway with unaccustomed ease and certainty.

Over to you! My fervent hope is that we should be fellow-travellers Home, along that same wide trunk road.

I don't think I can do better than conclude this chapter with two quotations from a teacher of mine. The first is: *I see only what you see, but I have trained myself to notice what I see,* and I take it from his case *The Blanched Soldier.* The second is: *When (my) deduction is confirmed by quite a number of independent incidents the subjective becomes objective, and we can say we have reached our goal,* and I take it from his case *The Sussex Vampire.*

That teacher is no longer around, but you can still visit Sherlock Holmes' apartment in Baker Street, London.

AFTERWORD

All it's complexities notwithstanding, the message of this book is SIMPLICITY itself—Look in and See that at Centre you are Nothing. Turn around and See that this Nothing explodes into Everything. Turn round again, go back to the Place you never really left, and See What's here. Then take what comes of that triple vision. It will be all right.